Can God Call a Woman to Pastor

By

Franklin E. Rutledge

This book is a work of non-fiction. Names and places have been changed to protect the privacy of all individuals. The events and situations are true.

ISBN: 1-4107-3578-8 (e-book)
ISBN: 1-4107-3577-X (Paperback)
ISBN: 1-4107-9315-X (Dust Jacket)

This book is printed on acid free paper.

1stBooks - rev. 08/06/03

Dedication:

In memory of my magnificent mother, Ola Mae Rutledge, who passed away on January 18, 2003. She was a woman of great Christian courage and strength. A one of a kind Proverbs 31 woman.

To my wonderful wife and my three children, who put up with me while I engaged myself to this book: Shiann, Tyrell, Michael and Jessica.

To my pastor Reverend Ruth Williams.

To my sister Mary Jean Fulgham and my brother-in-law Charles Fulgham for funding this book deal. I can't say thank you enough.

To the people of the small town of Wilton, Alabama, who always believed in me.

To all the women of God who have and are now allowing God to use them by his grace.

Thanks:

Thanks to the many people that encouraged me to write this book. Pastor Elaine Burke, who allowed me to teach many women seminars in the church where she pastors. My brother-in-law, Overseer Henry Robinson, who advised me to persevere at any cost. Bishop Eric Reynolds, who helped fulfilled a prophecy that was given to me in 1980 by Elder John Savage of Virginia; that I would help people understand their place in the body of Christ. It was at that time when I wanted to challenge another person concerning a woman's place in the ministry. Elder Savage was my pastor at that time. He advised me to wait because God would use me to help the body of Christ understand this issue. Bishop Reynolds was moved by God to invite me to discuss this issue on a local television station in Delaware. I had forgotten what Elder Savage said to me until I finished this book. (God is Faithful). My sister and friend in the Lord, Hazel Edmonds for her kind words of wisdom, encouraging me not to give up. Sister Janette Johnson, for reviewing my rough draft before sending the manuscript to the publishers.

Biography: All scriptures taken from the King James's Bible unless otherwise noted.

The Pilgrim's Progress.
Biological Anthropology – 3rd edition (Michael Alan Park).
Philo-Hendrickson Publishers 1993

Strong's Exhaustive concordance of the Bible – Holman Bible Publishers

Spiros Zodhiates – The Hebrew-Greek Key Study Bible – King James Version

Hastings Dictionary of the Bible – Hendrickson Publishers

Laying the Foundation – James Lee Beall

God couldn't be Everywhere?...So He made Mothers! Dr. Eugene Scott, Ph.D.

Psychology and Life-4th edition – Zimbardo-Gerrig

Introduction

I hope to show that a woman who has been saved by the power of Jesus Christ's blood, and who has been filled with the Spirit of God, can pastor a local church assembly. The truth of this discovery or incessant practice is not to put men down, nor to take away from their maleness. It is to show that God is in control of His Church, and any woman that God decides to use for his glory can be used, and that women who have accepted the Lord are in the body of Christ.

I also want to establish that circumstances are not the reason to believe that something is true. Just because I am under a woman pastor does not make women pastoring right. Nor does it make it right just because history tells of the countless number of women in the ministry. Just because women are successful in the ministry does not mean God approves of what they are doing. Personal success does not establish truth. Truth is not based on what you do, or what someone else does. It depends on principle. The principle that I stand upon is the word of God. His word must be studied objectively, not subjectively based on our denominational beliefs. The contents of what is written cannot be changed to fit our own personal philosophy. Its truth is not made known by our subjective feelings or beliefs. It is truth because it is truth, not because I believe it or not. It is truth.

At the end of this book, I want to introduce you to two women pastors in the State of Connecticut. One pastored the Pentecostal Assembly Church in Waterbury. The other pastors the Grace Apostolic Church of Jesus in Terryville. These women of God proved through the Holy Spirit that a woman could pastor a local assembly. Even when a woman is successful, it does not prove that God calls a woman to pastor. It must be God's position, and God's position alone that establishes truth.

Can God call a woman into the pastoral Ministry? - Prejudice

The question of whether a woman can preach is not a new one; it is as old as the church, which started in 30 A.D. One must understand that it was the Jewish men who were the front-runners of the church. That culture did not allow women to get an education, even though few women did serve in the temple. Luke 2:36-38 tells of a prophetess that serviced in the temple day and night. Her name was Anna. She served God with fasting and praying. She had the gift of prophecy. She may not have been allowed to serve in the temple sacrifices, or read the Law of Moses to the people, but God used her. She may not have been able to stand behind someone's wooden podium, but she was used of God.

Jesus chose twelve apostles to lay the foundation of the church. Matthew 10:2-4, "Now the names of the twelve apostles are these; the first, Simon, who is called Peter, and Andrew his bother; James the son of Zebedee, and John his brother; Philip, and Bartholomew; Thomas, and Matthew the publican; James the son of Alphaeus and Lebbaeus, whose surname was Thaddaeus; Simon the Canaanite, and Judas Iscariot, Who also betrayed him."

Let me pause here to highlight a point of God's grace and deliverance. If you noticed in the previous paragraph, one of the apostles was a Canaanite (Simon). In Genesis 9:24-27 we read, "And Noah awoke from his wine, and

1

knew what his younger son had done unto him. Moreover, he said, Cursed be Canaan; a servant of servants shall he be unto his brethren. He also said, blessed be the Lord God of Shem; and Canaan shall be his servant. God shall enlarge Japheth, and he shall dwell in the tents of Shem; and Canaan shall be his servant." According this scripture it was Noah who cursed Canaan, not God. Not all the sons of Ham were cursed. Canaan would serve his servant brethren. It was not until much later that the attitudes toward the Canaanites turn into hatred. Not because of the curse to be servants, but because the Israelites had to fight against them to regain their land. Jesus destroyed the prejudice attitude toward the Canaanites. Jesus had no respect to Noah's curse of the Canaanites, nor did he dishonor the Samaritans because the Jews hated them. God created man in his own image; free. If man had any curse placed upon him because of the works of the Devil, they are now set free through Christ Jesus.

Many people misread the Bible and concluded that Noah cursed Ham, therefore cursing the entire Negro ethnic group. Because of this curse, the Negro man or woman cannot be equal with an ethnic group that believes they are the superior group. This *"superior group"* does not believe that the ethnic group that came from Ham can preach the gospel. Prior to slaves of America owning their own churches, they were not allowed to sit with the white people in the same congregation. From the time the Europeans forced slavery on the African people, to American forced slavery of the same group, the label attached to the African black skinned people was that they were the cursed of God. The Bible does not teach this at all.

People, who accepted this philosophy, will also accept the philosophy that the wearing of head covering came from God (I Corinthians 11:1-16). There is no sublaw from the Law of Moses that required a woman to wear a head covering during the time of worship to show submission to her head. If it was a shame for women to speak in a church gathering, then what power did a head covering have to make exception to this rule of "keep silent"? If the power to prophesy comes from the Holy Spirit, then the Spirit can never work in a woman's life until she is covered. If God ever spoke through a woman without her head being covered, then it is not a requirement of God for head covering. If there is a law from God that dictates that a woman should have her head covered before she prophesies, and if a woman prophesied without her head covered, she has broken the whole law of God. James 2:10. My question then is, what sacrifice would she offer for this sin?

The tradition of head covering was a symbolic submissive respect from the wife to the husband. God said in the book of Ezekiel 11:19-20, "And I will give them one heart, and I will put a new spirit within you; and I will take the stony heart out of their flesh, and will give them a heart of flesh: That they may walk in my statutes, and keep mine ordinances, and do them: and they shall be my people, and I will be their God." In addition, in the Gospel of John 4:23 "But the hour cometh, and now is when the true worshippers shall worship the Father in Spirit and in truth: for the Father seekth such to worship him." Jesus said, "I am the way, the truth and the life…" John 14:6. The truth to get to God and his anointing is through the Lord Jesus Christ. Jesus excluded all material things and works as a prerequisite to gain the favor of God. The proper order for *anointing* with God is (1) accepting his Son Jesus Christ, (2) faith, (3) holiness and (4) whatever is requested of the Lord. In Luke 18:18-21 Jesus made it clear to the young pure man that lived a high moral life with all the trimmings connected to the law, that the way to the kingdom was to follow Him. All the things that he was doing were needful, but the kingdom could not be obtained through works. Therefore, demanding that women wear hats to show that they are submissive to man is ok for man. It does not indicate a relationship with God.

If a woman wants to show submission to her husband, she should do it with the heart as stated in I Peter 3:1-6. All symbols have future manifestations. The head covering is not a symbol of a submissive heart to God. Jesus Christ is the head of the Church. As hard and as difficult as my next statement may be to many, it is also true. "In Christ there is neither male nor female, therefore the man is not the head of the woman in Christ. Christ and Christ alone is the head of the Church." This being the case, head covering is not needed anymore as a symbol, because Christ has been manifested.

The Christian church should always have a standard that represents the holiness of God. That standard should not replace the saving grace of the Lord. If a local church assembly has a practice that persuades it member's profession of faith to include it practices for salvation or anointing, then they are accursed, Galatians 1:6-9. Grace frees a person from all works that make that person feels he or she is saved because they are doing these things. The Bible speaks of dead works – Hebrews 6:1. If God calls a person before they were separated from their mother's womb, what makes us think we will please God by wearing head covering? If you feel – personally – that, you have to wear head covering, then wear it. Nevertheless, do not think you are pleasing God. If we really want to please God in the time of grace, go out and witness to the unsaved, feed the hungry, visit those in prison, give the man or woman of God a drink of water, and feed the children who have no food to eat. Matthew 25:31-46.

Jesus asked a question to the crowd when they advised him that his mother, brothers and sisters were there to see him. Who are my mother, brother and sister, they that do the will of my father? Matthew 13:46-50 It is more dangerous to not feed the people of God than to wear a head covering.

No one is set free of cultural belief over night. These apostles were part of a cultural belief system that did not allow women to interact with men. We can see this attitude displayed with the woman at the well with whom Jesus was talking. (St. John 4:27) In addition, we can see an attitude of segregation in Peter toward other nationalities, Acts 10th chapter. We can also come to conclusion based on the scriptures that children were a part of this segregation and prejudice attitude. Can it be God's will that children are not allowed to be in the company of "men"? It can't be the will of God that children are pushed aside and ignored as though their brains have not developed to the point they can interact intelligently. Luke 18:16 "But Jesus called them unto him, and said, suffer little children to come unto me, and forbid them not: for such is the kingdom of God." Two children became kings in Judah: Uzziah – 16 years old (II Chronicles 26:1), and Josiah – 8 years old. Apparently, prejudice against women and children had set in the hearts of men over a period of time until they thought it was God's will for them to suppress this group. God had called Jeremiah before he came out of the womb. The hindrance for women and children was not from God, but the prejudice of men. It still exists today.

Many times, we true Christians think that people are delivered from years of prejudice over night. It takes time for God to work on us as we feed on his word. In a belief moment, the blood of Jesus Christ can eradicate the spiritual sinful nature. However, what has been living in our bodies takes time to get out. We can be born again of the word of God! I see prejudice in my own church organization and other church organizations by the comments that are made. Dr. Fred Price had to rebuke his majority black congregation for their attitudes toward whites. Charles Swindoll had to rebuke his majority white congregation for their attitudes toward blacks. Heaven, help us all.

We see in Acts 6:1-3 where the Grecian complained because their women were not used in the daily **ministration.** The Grecians women were ministers prior to their conversion to Christianity. When the Hebrew elders left them out of the ministry, the Grecian men and women took offense to this neglect. So we see, the problem with women preachers is a cultural thing, and not whether God has chosen them. The church had not come into the knowledge that God's government was ruled by Christ, and not by man. The Apostle Paul and the author of the book of Hebrews opened up this understanding to the brethren. They taught that the church was made up of spiritual beings, but these spiritual beings have been baptized into the spiritual body of Christ to do spiritual warfare with the spiritual enemy – Satan.

There are many people who do not believe that God calls a woman into the ministry of authority. The majority of these are men that head religious organizations (the places where the souls worship). Most of these men feel that it is God who set this standard, so they are following the plan of God. If we search the scriptures, we will find that it is not God, but rather the subjective feeling of the male gender that holds this as a standard from God.

Apostle Gino Jennings vs Bishop Eric Reynolds and Elder Franklin Rutledge

Below is an outline of my argument that was prepared for a debate against Apostle Gino Jennings. Apostle Jennings is the pastor of The Truth of God Ministries. His argument can be found on his websit www.truthofgod.com. I was invited by Bishop Eric Reynolds of New Castle, Delaware to participate in the live televised debate. Mr. Jenning did not show for the debate, but we had the dialogue on Monday, June 10, 2002. The original contents or this argument have been changed to reflect additional revealed information on this subject matter.

Argument:

Apostle Gino Jennings has stated without any apology, as if he heard from God himself, that God does not call a woman to pastor, preach or speak in the church. He also states that if any Christian woman pastor, preach or teach, she is going to hell. He also stated that if any man listens to a woman they are going to hell. In my argument, I want to show that God calls the Church. The Church is not called to load and unload heavy boxes. The Church is not called to run physical marathons. The Church is called to preach the Gospel of Jesus Christ. That only takes spirit and soul. Jesus said to the disciples "For it is not ye that speak, but the Spirit of your Father which speaketh in you." (Matthew

8

10:20) The question I would like to ask is, (1) was this for the Apostles only? (2) Am I included? (3) Are women included?

In the Gospel of John 17:20-21 "Neither pray I for these alone, but for them also which shall believe on me through their word; That they *all* may be one; as thou, Father, art in me, and I in thee, that they also may be one in us: that the world may believe that thou hast sent me." Question (1), did Jesus include women in this prayer? (2) If he did, are they one in a different way than what the men are supposed to be? (3) And, did Jesus mean for them to be one? Will the women have the same power in the spirit as the men?

Apostle Jennings posted his argument on the website. I have copied it exactly as he posted. This was printed off on December 12,2002. This is by no means to attack this man of God. It is his philosophy that we take issue with.

Women Preachers
Written By: Pastor Gino Jennings

Greetings Brothers, and Sisters, Friends, and Enemies. As touching the subject of Women Preachers, this has been a lie told in the land for many years, that God has called and sent Women to Preach! There's hundreds on hundreds of so-called women preachers, and all of them have the same lying mouth, that God sent them to preach. God never called or sent Women to Preach! You may wonder why I say that? Because there's no bible that says he did! Understand this, and get this well, there's no place in the bible where women did any preaching! Nowhere! The bible condemns women trying to preach and having authority over the man.

Now let us go to the Bible, and whatever the bible says, that's what we're going to take. anytime you read the truth in the bible and still don't believe it, then you are a plain hypocrite! Women and weak men try to justify themselves in the scriptures, but all have failed. One scripture they use is Numbers 22:27-28, "And when the ass saw the angel of the Lord, SHE fell down under Balaam: and Balaam's anger was kindled, and he smote the ass with a staff. And the Lord opened the mouth of the ass, and she said unto Balaam, what have I done unto thee, that thou hast smitten me these three times?" Out of ignorance, and the scripture says be not ignorant, they emphasize the fact that it was a female animal. Just because it spoke to Balaam they say that gives them the right to preach, because the women preachers compare themselves to a dumb ass or (donkey).

10

Get this women preachers, you've over looked what kind of voice came out the dumb ass. Notice II Peter 2:15-16, "Which have forsaken the right way, and are gone astray, following the way of Balaam the son of Boser, who loved the wages of unrighteousness; But was rebuked for his iniquity; the DUMB ASS SPEAKING WITH MAN'S VOICE forbad the madness of the prophet." As you can see the dumb ass spoke with man's voice, so you can't go to Numbers to justify yourself woman preacher.

The so-called women preachers also speak of Deborah because she judged Israel. That's true, but the bible didn't say she preached! Deborah was a prophetess and the fools and slow of heart try to tie that in with Joel 2:28, "And it shall come to pass afterward, that I will pour out my spirit upon all flesh; and your sons and your DAUGHTERS SHALL PROPHESY, you old men shall dream dreams, your young men shall see visions." Not knowing the scriptures nor the Power of God, they'll say prophesying is preaching. Prophesying is NOT preaching, but it's the foretelling of an event that's going to come. It's given to women to prophesy, but not to preach! St. Mark 16:9-10, "Now when Jesus was risen early the first day of the week, he appeared first to Mary Magdalene, out of whom he had cast seven devils. And she went and told them that had been with him, as they mourned and wept." The false churches and Devil built organizations love to tell a lie on this scripture by saying Mary preached the first message. You told a lie and everyone that believes that, believes a lie, because the bible didn't say she preached the first anything! You can always get a heathen to lie on God and his word!

11

Another scripture they always lie on is Galatians 3:28, "There is neither Jew nor Greek, there is neither bond nor free, there is neither male nor female: for ye are all one in Christ Jesus." From this scripture, the lie they tell is God will use a woman just like he'll se a man. The bible never made so such statement, so that's another lie. Galatians 3:28 is shewing that God has no respect of persons regarding salvation. The scripture says, "Then Peter opened his mouth, and said, of a truth I perceive that God is no respecter of persons. But in EVERY NATION he that feareth him, and worketh righteousness, is accepted with him." Acts 10:34-35. It says again, "For ye are ALL THE CHILDREN of God by faith in Christ Jesus." Galatians 3:26. Galatians 3:28 didn't have a thing to do with letting a woman preach The Gospel of Jesus Christ. When you're blind and deceived of the Devil, you'll believe every lie and damnable doctrine that comes along. Philippians 4:3, "And I entreat thee also, true yoke-fellow, help those women which labored with me in the gospel, with Clement also, and with other my fellow-labourers, whose names are in the Book of Life." When the Apostle Paul said, "Help those women which labored with me in the gospel", right then that old carnal mind will say he had women helping him preach, and of course that's not the truth. You didn't read about no woman helping Paul preach any-thing at any-time.

The Apostle Paul declared, "But though we, or an angel from heaven, preach any other gospel unto you than that which we have preached unto you, let him be accursed. As we said before, so say I now again, if any man preach any other gospel unto you then that ye have received, let him be accursed." Galatians 1:8-9. The Apostles forbid us to bring another Gospel that differ from what they preach. If they didn't allow women to preach then, nobody is justified in having them now! Notice Ecclesiastes 7:27-28, "Behold, this have I found, saith the preacher, counting one by one, to find out the account: Which yet my soul seeketh, but I find not: ONE MAN AMONG A THOUSAND HAVE I FOUND; but a WOMAN among all those have I NOT FOUND." King Soloman didn't find none in his day! Isaiah 3:12, As for my people, children are their oppressors, and WOMEN RULE OVER THEM. O my people, they which LEAD THEE CAUSE THEE TO ERR, AND DESTROY THE WAY OF THY PATH."

Reader, do you see what Isaiah is saying? He spoke plain here, that if a woman leads you she will cause you to err, and you'll be destroyed! Despite what the Bible says, you still have foolish, hell-bound, weak, ungodly men ordaining women for Bishops, Elders, Pastors, and Deaconess. You have women standing head of churches leading men and women to Hell fire and destruction. Isaiah 9:16-17, "For the LEADERS, of this people cause them to ERR, and they that are LED of them are DESTROYED. Therefore, the LORD SHALL HAVE NO JOY IN THEIR YOUNG MEN, neither shall have mercy on their fatherless and widows: For everyone is an HYPOCRITE and an EVIL DOER, and every mouth speaketh FOLLY. For all this his anger is not turned away, but his hand is stretched out still." Everyone that sits under women preachers are hypocrites and evil-doers, according to what the word of God says!

Some are fool enough to call themselves BISHOP! How wicked, and blind by the hands of the Devil. The bible says in I Timothy 3:1-2, "This is a true saying, (This lets us know, any other saying apart from this true saying is a lie!) If a MAN desire the office of a Bishop, HE (Not She) desireth a good work. A Bishop then must be blameless, the HUSBAND of one wife, (It didn't say the wife of one husband!) vigilant, sober, of good behavior, given to hospitality, apt to teach." Listen to what Paul said, "Let your women keep SILENCE in the churches: For it is NOT PERMITTED unto them to SPEAK; but they are commanded to be under obedience, as also saith the law. And if they will learn anything, LET THEM ASK THEIR HUSBANDS AT HOME: for it is a SHAME FOR A WOMAN TO SPEAK IN THE CHURCH." I Corinthians 14: 34-35.

You find so-called women preachers going contrary to the bible, and having speaking appointments. Even though the bible says for them to be silent in the churches, and if they want to know anything ask their husbands at home, they willingly ignore The Bible and still insist on standing before the church and tell their husbands and everyone else what to do. You've got to be a hypocrite to ignore the Bible! I Timothy 2:11-14, "Let the woman learn in silence with all subjection. But I suffer not a woman to teach, nor to usurp authority over the man, but to be in silence. For Adam was first formed, then Eve. And Adam was not deceived, but the woman being deceived was in the transgression." As you can plainly see, the scriptures are against women preachers. The bible only allows the aged women to teach the younger women according to Titus 2:3-4-5, "The aged women likewise, that they be in behavior as becometh holiness, not false accursers, not given to much

14

wine, teachers of good things; (Now the bible is going to outline what the woman is to teach, and she's not to go no further.) that they may teach the YOUNG WOMEN to be sober, to love their husbands, to love their children, to be discreet, chaste, keepers at home, good, obedient to their husbands, that the word of God be not blasphemed." When women follow that, then they are in keeping with what the Word of God says. "Let all things be done decently and in order." I Corinthians 14:40.

In my conclusion Brothers and Sisters, you don't have Women Apostles, or Women Bishops or Elders or Pastors or Evangelists or Deaconesses in the Bible! It's of the Devil and out of the Pit of hell! All churches that have women preachers or believe in Women Preachers, you don't believe the bible and your worship is in VAIN. My advice to you reader is come out of every church that have women preachers, and walk with The Truth.

Revelations 2:20, "Notwithstanding I have a few things AGAINST THEE, Because thou sufferest that woman Jezebel, which called herself a prophetess, to TEACH and to seduce my servants to commit fornication, and to eat things sacrificed with idols."
These were some of the questions I was prepared to ask Apostle Jennings if the debate had taken place.

Response to a yes answer: So what you are saying is that it is not out of the character of God to call a woman to be a pastor. Therefore, a woman can be a pastor.

Response to a no answer: Are you saying God is not sovereign and that he is limited in His power? God does not have all power. Which means he is not Lord? No man can say he is Lord, but by the Holy Ghost. Therefore, if the Holy Ghost is in a person, that person has to say that God can call a woman to pastor-because He can do all things. If a person say God cannot call a woman to pastor, then that person is not speaking from the Holy Ghost but by the devil. Because the Lord Himself asks the question in Genesis 18:14 "Is any thing too hard for the Lord?"

Are you saying there are things that God cannot do? Which means it is out of His character to do those things? If you are saying that God cannot call a woman into the pastoral ministry, then what you are saying is that (1) there has never been a time in the history of man that a woman was called into a leadership role by God where men were under them. (2) There must not be an event in history when a woman ruled over a man.

We know that it is not in the character of God to lie. I Samuel 15:29; Numbers 23:19; Malachi 3:6 support this fact. Therefore, we much establish that it is not in the character of God to call a woman into the position of leadership over the man. If he did, then He is a liar. Therefore, everything He says is a lie. If he is a liar, then he does not exist as the atheists have stated. Therefore, we are all without hope.

Definitions

The word pastor from a biblical definition: The Greek word poimen means shepherd. Designation for a spiritual leader of the flock. One who has authority. Ephesians 4:11 "and he gave some apostles, and some prophets and some evangelists, and some pastors, and teachers."

Where does ministry of pastoring come from? Is it a gift from God or man?

A. It is a spiritual gift from God to the body of Christ. Ephesians 4:8-13.

B. It does not have male or female designation like deacons or bishops. These offices are clearly designated for men. I Timothy 3:1-13.

C. There is neither male nor female in the body. Galatians 3:23-29. He sets in the body as it pleases him. I Corinthians 12:18. Christ is the head of the body and we are members. Ephesians 5:23.

D. The gender female can receive the gift of pastoring because she is in the body. I Corinthians 12:22-23.

Preacher: *kerusso and prokusso* to proclaim, herald, to cry.

Preach: the action of a preacher - there are many types of preachers: preacher of righteousness, preacher of medicine, preacher of abortion and many others. In the field of law they have their bible - they that are of this field preach law.

Witness - someone who communicates to someone else what they have seen or heard. Anyone who is a witness for Christ, be it male or female, have been told by the ones they are witnessing to, "don't preach to me." Therefore, if you are a witness, then you are a preacher.

Prophetess: *Naviah* - A woman that speaks for the Lord.

Prophet: *Navi* - A man that speaks for the Lord.

Prophesy: *nava, Nvuah* – To speak while being lead by the Lord. To proclaim present and future.

Bishop: *Episkope* - Inspection, superintendence
Episkeptomal - To go to see, relieve, to out, visit
Episkopeo - **Look diligently, take the oversight**

Apostle – *Apostollos* – Sent one, messenger, ambassador

Deacon - *Diako* – To run on errands; an attendant-waiter, teacher and pastor

(Deacon or Deaconess) - *Diakoneo* – to use the office of.

License - A piece of paper given to a member of an organization to testify that the member has the right to act in the name of that organization. It gives rights to the member.

Ordain - to approve of the power that has been given to work in the stead of. To lay hands on for specific service.

Anoint - to empower for service to act in the stead of.

Church - ekklesia (the ones called out). The spiritual kingdom of God through Christ Jesus. The people that will inherit the kingdom of God. The ones that obey the ethics of Christ Jesus.

God's Plan for the Female

Was it the plan of God for the woman to be in authority over man?

Genesis 1:26-28. God created male and female in his image and after his likeness. He gave **_them_** the dominion over the fish of the sea and over the fowl of the air, and over every living thing that moves upon the earth.

They would rule over all that were, that should come and are on the earth. This was God's plan for male and female, because they were created by God as one ruling power. God called them Adam. Genesis 5:1-2 - the same in created authority.

The Devil came and brought sin into the world. Now, the woman knows good and evil. God strips her of her power to rule with the male. Her desires will be toward her husband. She did not respect God as her ruler; therefore, she shall be ruled over by her husband. The works of the Devil had started.

Nevertheless, Jesus who is the second Adam was manifested to take away our sins and destroy the works of the Devil. I John 3:5-8; Romans 5:14. He destroyed the works of the Devil freeing us to enter into the holy of holiest as one; male and female. Then he gave gifts unto the church, which is his body (Ephesians 4:8-13). Now through Jesus Christ, the women can rule-in sainthood-with the man. She no longer sits around while men are having coffee and speaking of the deep things of God. Jesus stopped all

20

that by telling Martha she need to do the best thing, not just service to men but the best thing (Luke 10:39-42). This is a mystery about women being set free from the traditions of men; freed to do the work of the Lord.

Paul encourages the single males and females not to marry. By staying single, you have the world at your disposal without the fear of wondering when your possessive husband or wife will tell you not to do certain things. A single male or female that loves God is able to serve him to the utmost. They don't have to worry about using their money for the ministry. They don't have to worry about what time to be in the house. They do not have to worry about not fasting and praying. They are totally free to <u>serve</u> the Lord. As the words taken from the Lion's King song go, "no body says do this, no body says be there, and no body says stop this." God can use a person that is not under bondage (I Corinthians 7:32-34). What I want you to see from this scripture is that God uses females, especially if they are single.

The truth of God's word is hide from the simple. Simple-minded people are culturally based. They will only read and repeat the portion of God's word that fits into their personal belief or their church doctrine.

A Woman

What is woman? Moreover, why is it that men say they "will not be under her control in business or in a religious institutional setting?" Is it her make up, her voice, or her historical setting?

Genesis 2:21-23 "And the Lord God caused a deep sleep to fall upon Adam, and he slept; and he took one of his ribs, and closed up the flesh instead thereof; and the rib, which the Lord God had taken from man, made he a woman, and brought her unto the man. In addition, Adam said, "this is now bone of my bones, and flesh of my flesh: she shall be called Woman, because she was taken out of Man." For those of us who are convinced by faith that God created the woman in his image, it is easy to establish this one fact; that she is part of the male, and the male is part of her.

The rib is considered one of the strongest parts of mankind's anatomy. It protects the lungs, the heart and the kidney. Philo, the Jewish philosopher, wrote concerning why God took one of the man's ribs and made woman. "Indeed our ribs are like sisters, and akin in all parts, and they consist of flesh.... Ordinary custom calls the ribs, which is equivalent to saying that he has vigour (vigor). A wrestler has strong ribs - he is strong. Harp players have ribs - he has energy and power in his playing."

God made the woman to be strong. Philo also describes her as the "outward sense of the soul." She is the burden bearer. She carries all the duties that are demanded by the soul. She is the body of the soul: legs, feet, arms and hands. She does all the housework, taking care of children and the husband. She cannot get tired or sick. However, if she does, she must be strong enough to take care of everybody else. She has to think for everybody; honey where is this. Mommy have you seen my ****? Honey, what time are we supposed to be there, and where are we supposed to go? This, my fellow male friend, equates to the woman being strong.

This excerpt is taken from the book "god couldn't' be Everywhere?...So He Made Mothers!" by Dr. Gene Scott, Ph D. "In the Scofield Reference Bible, women are described as being created in the image of God that relates to his ability to nurture. *"The etymological signification of Almighty God (El-Shaddia) is both interesting and touching. God (El) signifies the "Strong One"... The qualifying word Shaddai is formed from the Hebrew word "shad," the breast; e.g. Genesis 49:25; Job 3:12; Psalm 22:9; Song of Solomon 1:13; 4:5; 7:3-8; 8:1-10; Isaiah 28:9; Ezekiel 16:7. Shaddai therefore means primarily "the breasted." God is "Shaddai," because He is the Nourisher, the Strength-giver, and so, in a secondary sense, the Satisfier, who pours Himself into believing lives. As a fretful, unsatisfied babe is not only strengthened and nourished from the mother's breast, but also is quieted, rested, satisfied, so El Shaddai is that name of God which sets Him forth as the Strength-giver of His people."

The woman represents the motherly part of God. Job 21:24 "His breasts are full of milk, and his bones are moistened with marrow." The breasts are to nurture a child to keep them satisfied. God is the satisfier of his people. Like a mother, he brings contentment to his people. God's love is displayed in the love of mothers. "You women thought you had those breasts so men could say how wonderful you look." Not so. Females have a character behind the breasts that we men see as pleasurable and exciting. This character holds nations, communities and families together. Without this breasted species, there would be an unbalanced emotion among the human race. We would all be head strong and uncaring, at least outwardly. This type of nurturing character brings peace and harmony. A family is made up of male and female. No one will ever doubt that there are circumstances where a child has to be raised by the mother or father alone. There are times when the grandparents will raise the child. There are times when a single grandmother or grandfather will raise the child. There are times when siblings will raise siblings. However, no child should be raised with the attitude that he or she does not need both the male and the female as a rearing factor. I was raised in a community where families raised each other's families. We learned, because of the male and female presence, to respect our elders. It was the character of the women that held us together before we became adults and decided that good living was not worth it. We looked at the type of men we had as role models and figured that it is ok to drink alcohol, fight, and gamble, beat your wife and smoke cigarettes. The women built character while the men instilled fear and respect. "Add that together." When a woman displays her God given nurturing spirit in leadership, it fosters cohesiveness among the members of a congregation. Women are better at showing this side of the Creator. She is like God who is the breasted one. God is not weak because he has these characteristics, and I don't believe women leaders are weak because they have these character traits from God.

Are Women Autonomous?

Genesis 3:16, "Unto the woman he said I will greatly multiply thy sorrow and thy conception; in sorrow thou shall bring forth children; and thy desire shall be to thy husband, and he shall rule over thee." Did God take away the woman or wife's free will at this time?

Desire; tesh-oo-kaw. A longing (Strong Exhaustive concordance).
Tshuqah. Stretching out after, a yearning, a longing, a desire (The Hebrew – Greek Key Study Bible).

According to these definitions, the wife's desire is to long for her husband. She is to depend on him in an emotional way. She should see to it that *she* satisfies him. She should long for *her* husband only. This definition the man and the woman understood, because they were just coming out of the stage of innocence. Their minds were not filled with the tradition of the religions that treated women, as if they were nothing. God did not give them a road map as to what "your desires to your husband" meant. They knew, and it is my belief that the man did not treat the woman as if she did not have a free will.

Rule; mashal. Part of Eve's punishment was submission to the appropriate leadership of her husband over the family.

Before man (male and female) failed God, they were equal in their own eyes and in the eyes of God. They were

26

naked and not ashamed. They were innocent in the sight of the Lord. Both of them understood their roles in the created work of God; they were the Church. This was the government of man from God. As they procreated, the seeds that came from them would be the worshippers that would inherit the earth. Under the spirit of innocence, everyone understood his or her roles or places.

When sin came into the world and man's (male and female) hearts no longer worked in harmony, God stepped in and gave marching orders. "Adam you are first. Eve you are second. Neither one of you now know how to lead, so Adam, you work by the sweat of your face for your family. Eve, your desires will be toward your husband, and he will be your leader. My government will be in your husband's hands until the Christ shall come. He will restore all things back to me. Moreover, you will work together again. Satan will distort the truth, as you already have experience. Everything will be out of whack until the coming of the Christ. Nevertheless, I will watch over you and cover you. Best wishes." (Quote and interpretation mine.) If you notice when God was speaking to Adam, he did not tell him how to rule over the woman. He did not tell the man to make her submit to him. He told Eve that the job of submission would be her responsibility. He did not tell Adam to make her submit. Sarah called Abraham lord because he never required that honor. (Supposition mine)

It is safe to state this fact concerning our attempt to handle God's things; sin distorts any order that God gives us. Man, in his sinful state, cannot rule righteously. Solomon ruled the kingdom wisely but not righteously. God did not intend for man to misunderstand the orders that he gave to the woman. God's order was not for the man to take away the woman's autonomy. He was not to prevent her from getting an education, or prevent her from getting a job to help her husband. God did not intend for the woman to become a slave. God did not intend for man's rulership to include ordering the woman to wear a veil over her face, and to walk five paces behind him while she holds the baby and the baby bags. Ruled over does not mean that rulers can slap, punch or kick the wife. It means that the ruler is to lead you in righteousness. It is to bring positive attitude into the family so the male and the female off springs will understand their role in life (Ephesians 5:25-29). We need to be born again.

Born again means change from the old attitude of sinful habits and man made traditions, to the attitude of Christ. Ephesians 2:5-7 "Let this mind be in you, which was also in Christ Jesus. Who, being in the form God thought it not robbery to be equal with God. But made himself of no reputation, and took upon him the form of a servant, and was made in the likeness of men:" When we are born again, we can see, think and act according to the spiritual law of God. The mind of God regarding how men should treat women cannot be found on the outside of the Holy Scriptures (Ephesians 5:22-32). This was always God's plan (I Corinthians 7:29-31). Submissiveness does not mean to take away autonomy.

If we follow Christ, our character should reflect the character of Christ (Psalm 119:137; Ezra 9:15). Righteousness is freedom. Unrighteousness is slavery. For any man to say that a woman cannot exercise her God given right of autonomy, means he doesn't believe God gave all mankind freewill. The law of righteousness governs Freewill. The law of righteousness is in the heart of every child of God, the governor and the governed. Each one of us are to act responsibly toward those in leadership positions (Hebrews 13:7,17).

Some time ago, a male friend of mine told me, that if he told his wife to get up at 3:00 A.M., go to the store and buy something for him, she should do it. If it is for no other reason than because he is her husband, she should get up and do it. I am serious - he told me that. Women, he is not the only one out here that feels that way. This person confesses that the Spirit of God dwells in his heart. This type of attitude cannot discern what true leadership is about. No true Christian man, that loves his wife, will request that she do such a thing to please him just because he is the husband. Once again, men ought to love their wives as Christ loved the Church. Jesus never sent his disciples any place without a purpose. In addition, because he was God, he was always with them. Improper training is the reason people do things like this.

Women are not slaves. They should be treated like the creature God created them to be. No matter what their positions are in life: mother, wife, daughter, girlfriend or single, they are still autonomous.

The Spiritual Mind

I have been stating throughout this book that the Church is spiritual. Jesus told Nicodemus that a man cannot see the kingdom of God until he is born again, St. John 3:3. The things of the kingdom cannot be known by the natural man. Romans 8:5 "For they that are after flesh do mind the things of the flesh; but they that are after the Spirit the things of the Spirit." I Corinthians 2:14-16 "But the natural man receiveth not the things of the Spirit of God: for they are foolishness unto him: neither can he know them, because they are spiritually discerned. However, he that is spiritual judgeth all things, yet he himself is judged of no man. For who hath known the mind of the Lord, that he may instruct him. But we have the mind of Christ." Holy men of God wrote the Bible, as they were move by the Holy Ghost. II Peter 1:20-21 "Knowing this first that no prophecy of the scripture is of any private interpretation. For the prophecy came not in old time by the will of man: but holy men of God spake as they were moved by the Holy Ghost." Not even the prophets understood what they spoke many times while in the spirit. The Bible is not a book to be understood by the general public. It is a foolish thing for a bible scholar, bible society, theologian, or a bible college to author a bible that is easy for the nature man to understand. People are trying to remove gender from the Holy Bible so that it will fit into the mainstream thought of political correctness. In social psychology, people are taught not to use the word policeman when you have a female police. This would be correct out of respect to the female officer. We should address her as policewoman or officer. You should recognize and respect the fact she is not a male. Society wants to remove singular gender title so genders will be honored. When you see the title man, it means man. When you see the title woman, it means woman. Every televisions, radio and printed media have to say he or she. Not so with the Bible. When the Bible uses the term "man", it is speaking about humanity, unless there is a specific name of people the Lord or the prophet is addressing. When the Bible uses the title "children", it speaks of a group of people related to another. It speaks of the character of a group of people. (Romans 8:16:17; I Corinthians 14:20; Ephesians 4:2-3; I Peter 1:14; I Peter 2:14).

When the Bible uses the title "sons", it speaks of a male seed or a created being by God. It speaks of power and authority. It speaks of "that" which is begotten of man or God. (Galatians 4:7; II Thessalonians 2:3; Genesis 6:2-4; Romans 8:14-19; I Corinthians 6:18; Galatians 4:5-6; Philippians 2:15; I John 3:1-2).

God does not have daughters. Men have daughters and sons. God has only sons. When the title son is in direct relationship with God it is a symbol of power and authority. There are times when this title refers to the entire Church. Some want to change it to sons and daughters, which cannot be done because God is not dealing with flesh and blood. So the Bible cannot be rewritten to speak the language of gender. We cannot add or take away from God's word to make it easy for people that cannot understand the spirit of the word of God. The title sons cannot be replaced with sons and daughters to please and comfort the natural minded reader.

I am not a theologian or bible scholar, but I do have the Spirit of God and I have studied the Word of God extensively over the last 25 years. I am very familiar with the spirit and context of the Bible and how it should read. God is immutable. There is consistency from Genesis through Revelations. Examples: The title virgin should never read young lady. A virgin can be a young lady, but a young lady doesn't necessarily have to be a virgin. When speaking about the mother of Jesus and Joseph, it should never read Jesus' parents. Joseph was not Jesus father. Therefore, Jesus did not have human blood (Acts 20:28). If he had human blood, he could not save us from our inherited sins. If Joseph is thought to be the father of Jesus, then we are still in our sins. The New Age Movement would love for this to be true. Therefore, no Bible should ever read that Joseph was Jesus' father.

New American Standard, Williams and the Beck Bibles translate Luke 2:33, "His father and his mother were surprised such things were said about Him."

The King James Bible translates this verse, "And Joseph and his mother marvelled at those things which were spoken of him."

Williams New Testament translates Matthew 1:18, "Now the birth of Christ Jesus occurred under these conditions.... she was found to be an expectant mother through the *influence* of the Holy Spirit." The devil influence Eve, but did not put the fruit in her mouth. The Holy Spirit overshadowed Mary and put the sperm in her womb. The angel influenced Mary to accept God's blessing on her. In an attempt to make the Bible easier to read and less hard to understand, they have put Jesus on our sinful level.

The reason for this chapter is help the child of God understand that the Bible is for the spiritual minded to understand. A person on the outside of Christ can memorize the entire Bible. They may be able to quote scriptures like an orator, but understand it like Queen Candace's eunuch (Acts 8:27). No man on the outside of Christ can instruct the Church on who should and who should not lead in God's house. The Church is the kingdom of God. The natural minded person can't see with understanding what goes on in the house of God. Flesh cannot see the things of God. I am afraid that too many of God's children are trying to lead by the flesh. It is not pleasing to God. Revelation from God is an awesome thing to behold when Spirit intercourse with spirit. If you try to understand a woman's position in the church by the flesh, you will miss it every time. Thank God we all can now go inside the Most Holy Place where the spirit of the Lord resides.

Is the male's brain better than the female's?

In anthropology we study the cranial capacity of Homo sapiens (humans) and Apes (non-humans). The difference between us is the brain sizes. (This is what the evolutionists say.) If the brain size is below 1200, they are non Homo sapiens. They may look like us, in some form or another, but they cannot act intelligent like us. I did not say that they are not intelligent; I said they are not like us. They cannot write and utter human sounds to communicate with us Homo sapiens. We can communicate with them. They cannot design and build bridges. They cannot rebuild to maintain life for all species. The things that non-humans can do, we have invented machines to do better.

In psychology, we study the brain to learn more about our motor skills, our cognitive ability, our sensory capability, and our emotions. In Human beings, male and female, the brain capability is the same.

The following information was taken from the Washington Faculty web site.
Bigger - Stronger - Faster...are there really any differences between female brains and male brains? Boys are between 12-20% larger than that of girls. The head circumference of boys is also larger (2%) than that of girls. However, when the size of the brain is compared to body weight at this age, there is almost no difference between boys and girls. Therefore, a girl baby and a boy baby who weigh the same will have similar brain sizes.

In adults, the average brain weight in men is about 11-12% MORE than the average brain weight in women. Men's heads are also about 2% bigger than women's are. Remember though, men on average weigh more than women and that <u>absolute brain size may not be the best measure of intelligence</u>. Many behavioral differences have been reported for men and women. For example, it has been said that women are better in certain language abilities and men are better in certain spatial abilities. Many studies have tried to find differences in the right and left cerebral hemispheres to suggest that male and female brains are different. However, few of these experiments have found meaningful differences between men and women. If fact, there are many <u>similarities</u> between the cerebral hemispheres of men and women. Differences between the brains of men and women have generated considerable scientific and public interest. If there are differences in the way that men and women behave, then it is reasonable to suppose that their brains have something to do with these behavioral differences. Just what are these differences and where in the brain these differences might be located.

For hundreds of years, scientists have searched for differences between the brains of men and women. Early research showing that male brains were larger than female brains was used to "prove" that male brains were superior to female brains. Of course, this "proof" is not so simple and straight forward as you will see. Nevertheless, even today, there is plenty of controversy about the differences in the brains of men and women. Not only from an anatomical point of view, but also from a functional point of view - in other words, just what do the differences in the brains mean?

Hormones that are present during a baby's development will affect the brain and determine whether the brain will be female or male. Studies that have looked at differences in the brains of males and females have focused on End of web-site information on the brain.

Almost all studies show that at birth, a boy's brain is bigger than a girl's brain. At birth, the average size of the brain for both boys and girls is the same. The capabilities of the brain for both sexes are the same. The only difference between the sexes is the hormone system, which will be discussed, in another book. Alternatively, you can listen to Dr. James Dobson. He is excellent on the subject of differences between the male and the female hormone system. The brains for both sexes have the following: left and right hemisphere joined by the corpus calosum. The left hemisphere carries spontaneous speaking and writing, response to complex commands, word recognition, memory for words and numbers, sequences of movements, positive emotion. The right hemisphere carries repetitive but not spontaneous speaking, responses to simple commands, facial recognition, memory for shapes and music, spatial interpretation, negative emotion and emotional responsiveness.

John Stuart Mill in his defense of women in The Subjection of Women, Chapter III, page 10 - wrote in the middle 1800s, "But (it is said) there is a anatomical evidence of the superior mental capacity of men compared with women: they have a larger brain. I replied that in the first place the fact itself is doubtful. It is by no means established that the brain of a woman is smaller than that of a man. If it is inferred, merely because a woman's bodily frame generally is of less dimensions than a man's this criterion would lead to strange consequences. A tall and large-boned man must on this showing be wonderfully superior in intelligence to a small man, and an elephant or a whale must prodigiously excel mankind...It is certain that some women have as large a brain as any man, it is with my knowledge that a man who had weighed many human brains, said that the heaviest he knew of, heavier even that Cuvier's (the heaviest previously recorded), was that of a woman."

From this study, I believe the males and females have the same intellectual abilities to function in the things pertaining to the brain. Therefore, whatever job involves the use of the brains, such as leadership, planning and others, both males and females are capable of achieving. I think males have problems with the physical makeup of females. They cannot look beyond what the Apostle Peter call the weaker vessel, I Peter 3:7. Peter did not state that the women were weak. He stated that her vessel was weak.

Would you call Jezebel weak; she made Elijah run to the wilderness. Would you call Delilah weak; she took Samson's strength. Would you call Moses' sister Miriam weak; she persuaded Aaron to go against Moses. Would you call Deborah weak; she judged Israel. Peter is referring to the woman's muscle structure (her frame). This was at a time when the culture would not allow women to have any say in religious matters or politics.

Physically it would be foolish for a woman to think she can endure the rigidity that a man's body can stand. A woman would be asking for an early physical break down if she continuously subject her body to heavy lifting. She is not made for this type of burdens. However, there are the exceptions. I know of women who are physically stronger than some men are. Women may be able to manage a male boxer, but never spar with him. Managing has nothing to do with what physical size you are; it has everything to do with how smart you are. Smartness comes from the brain, not the arms.

At the age of 24, I ended my enlisted tour with the United State Military and started my new life in the civilian world. The best managers I had were females. Compared to the males I was under, they had better organizational skill, better communication skills, and they related better with the employees. Except they tried to prove themselves more than the men. This statement is not to validate that women are called of God because of my experience with their good leadership. Truth is not based on circumstances, therefore this statement is to validate that I believe women can use their God given ability, which comes from their brain, to be good leaders.

With all of this brainpower, I can see why the man in the movie Yentl said, "she has no eternal spirit and soul. She can't read and write." "Brooms for women and books for men." I can clearly see why men from the eastern countries and in the United States want to keep women from getting an education and becoming leaders. They are afraid that they will be out done, because women do not get as tired as men do, and can remember much more than the men. "She is called the burden bearer."

What You See Is Not Always What You Get

A woman is beautiful. Whether she is black, white, yellow, brown or red, she is beautiful. Whether she is tall, short, skinny, or fat, she is beautiful.

God created her to be beautiful to us men. However, her physical beauty does not take away from her intellectual ability. Her beauty has caused her to sometimes take advantage of the weakness of the male species when she herself has lost her esteem (Proverbs 23:26-28). Maybe, this is one of the reasons men do not believe that God calls a woman to pastor a local church assembly.

Men look at women as objects to have sexual intercourse. I, as a man, should look at women this way. (They should not look to their own sex for this pleasure.) Maybe this is one of the reasons men cannot accept women as leaders. Some men feel that the women much meet their every need, have sexual intercourse, have babies and sweep the floor. While this is part of her responsibility as a good wife and mother, she is more than this. One of my women friends stated to me that she was tired of men looking at her as a sex object. I said, "sorry honey." You are a very pretty woman, and men are going to always look at you like that. But, you have to establish that you are more than a pretty body. Make men respect you as a gifted human being with a cranial capacity size over 1200 cc., especially because she is a godly saved woman.

When Samuel the prophet was looking for the next king of Israel, he was told by God to go to the house of Jesse.

When Samuel saw the tall robust healthy sons of Jesse, he thought surly God has called one of them. They looked like men of war. But God said I do not choose after the outward appearance (I Samuel 16:6-8). If God chooses by the heart, does he look at the gender? If he chose by the gender, is he saying that our hearts are not the same? I will say that the hearts of males and females are the same. It is not by power, nor by might, but its by the Spirit of the Lord (Zechariah 4:4-9).

If we look at the physical makeup of humanity - male and female - in the church and the work or God, we can be fooled by appearances. Many mighty men were not capable physically of accomplishing what they accomplished because of the strength in their frail bodies. God defeated the enemies.

A. Moses – Parted up the Red Sea, and closed it after the Egyptian army were in the midst of it, with a rod.
B. Joshua – With the priest and other people of Israel shouted the walls of Jerico down.
C. Deborah – The wife of Lapidoth judged Israel. For all the people who want to know if God ever called a woman to be over her husband, here is your answer – the prophetess Deborah. She Lead her General Barak to victory over Sisera.
D. Gideon – Defeated an army of two nations with only three hundred men; the numbers of the enemy were like grasshoppers.
E. Samson – Samson defeated the Philistines with the jawbone of an ass.

   F. David – The young lad defeated the loin, and the bear. Then he defeated the nine foot nine inch giant Goliath, by the power of the living God of Israel.

You may say that all these were men, except one. It shows that God only use men. My answer to this is that it was God with them that did the work. We must focus on what God can do. As God told Abram, "is there anything too hard for God?"

Were there ever times in the Bible when a Woman ruled over a Man?

Deborah – She judged Israel – Her husband was with her in Israel. Judges is a book that shows judges as authority. Judges 4:4

Miriam – One would have to conclude that she had authority, by the questions she raised to Aaron. Numbers 12:2

Phebe – a servant of the church at Cenchrea - Romans 16:1-2. Paul says of Phebe,
  1. Servant of the Church.
  2. Receive her in the Lord.
  3. Assist her - do whatever she ask you to do (literally to obey).
  4. She is a succourer - an assistant - one who has authority.

In Romans 1:1, Titus 1:1, James 1:1 and Jude 1st verse, Paul wrote to the men pastors of the church using the same word for serve as he did for Phebe. If the word is the same for both males and females, then the office is the same, making them equal in ministry.
In Romans 16:1-9, I Peter 3:7 Romans 16:21 and Philippians 1:24 we see men and women serving together.

Priscilla – is mentioned with Aquila, her husband, as having equal authority. Acts 18:1-2, 26-27; 19:1; I

Corinthians 1:12; 16:12. Was this not the original plan of God in Genesis 1:28 and Genesis 5:2.

As an elderly man, the Apostle John had a unique way of addressing the church members. He called them children. He also called those that were under another's authority in the local churches, children. In the following scriptures, we can distinguish between pastors and lay members by how John addressed them.

I John 2: My little children. 18th verse little children. 3:7 Little children. 18th verse My little children. 4:4 Ye are of God, little Children. 5:21 Little Children. This salutation of John, revealed that these members were under his spiritual care.

In John's third epistle, he writes to a pastor. Verse 4 "I have no greater joy than to hear that my children walk in truth."

In his second epistle, he writes to a woman – He addresses the church as her children. II John 1,4, 13. "The elder unto the elect lady and her children, whom I love in the truth and not I only, but also all they that have known the truth...I rejoiced greatly that I found of thy children walking in truth, as we have received a commandment from the Father...the children of thy elect sister greet thee. Amen."

In this second epistle of John, he addresses the church in the same manner in respect to authority. The church members are her children. He is consistent in acknowledging the church as children, while revealing to us the one that was in charge. In essence, the elect woman is the pastor.

The command from the scriptures is for all of us to submit ourselves. Hebrews 13:17 "obey them that have the rule over you, and submit yourselves: for they watch for your souls as they that must give account, that they may do it with joy, and not with grief: for that is unprofitable for you. Paul clearly tells the brethren of the church in Romans to submit themselves to Phebe. This is a woman ruling over men.

Were priests pastors?

The priests were the pastors in the Old Testament. Their jobs were to spiritually feed the flock of God, while the judges and kings ruled the land. The High Priest in general was the mediator between God and man. Exodus 29:1; II Chronicles 15:3; Micah 3:11; Ezekiel 1-2.

In the New Testament, the church is the priesthood. I Peter 2:9-10 "But ye are a chosen generation, a royal priesthood, a holy nation, a peculiar people, that ye should show forth the praises of him who has called you out of darkness into his marvelous light."

1. Is this scripture for the men of the church, or does it include women? If it includes women, then they can be shepherds of God's flock. If it does not include women, then God has not chosen them at all and they are still in darkness.

2. If priests have authority then women in the church can have authority.

3. In II Kings 22:11-17, it mentions the prophetess Huldah. God spoke through her to the king. She said, "thus saith the Lord." The word of the Lord came to pass. The king did not see the destruction that God caused to come upon the land. God said he would die an honorable death before that terrible day. After the king died, Nebuchadnezzar, king of Babylon came against Judah to destroy it.

46

The *woman's* word came to pass. Are we still saying God does not use a woman, or is this a true bible story. Let God be true and every man a liar. If this woman had not used the phrase that confirms prophecy, "thus saith the Lord, you could easily say she was speaking on her own. The word that she spoke came true, therefore God uses women.

Were Disciples Preachers?

Jesus chose twelve disciples and many other people became his disciples because of the miracles he preformed. He named the ones he had chosen Apostles. His message to them and all the disciples that saw him after his resurrection was to preach the gospel to every creature. It is the job of Christ's disciples to preach. No one can deny this truth.

Jesus sent the seventy disciples throughout all Judaea to preach, teach and to cast out devils. (1) The question I have for all my fellow male preachers is this, are all disciples commanded to preach to the world? If yes, then are saved women disciples? (2) If the Bible list women as disciples, then the next question is, did Jesus command the women not to preach? (3) Another question, does God hear all of his disciples?

Answers:
(1)   All disciples are commanded to preach the gospel. Mark 16:17 "And these signs shall follow them that believe; In my name shall hey cast out devils; they shall speak with new tongues;" Luke 10:1-1-2,17 "After these things the Lord appointed other seventy also, and sent them two and two before his face into every city and place, whither he himself would come. Therefore said he unto them, The harvest truly is great, but the labourers are few: pray ye therefore the Lord of the harvest, that he would send forth labourers into his harvest…and the seventy returned

again with joy, saying, Lord, even the devils are subject unto us through thy name."

(2)   Acts 9:36 "Now there was at Joppa a certain disciple named Tabitha, which by interpretation is called Dorcas: This woman was full of good works and almsdeeds which she did." Jesus did not say only male disciples are to take the gospel to the world, he said disciples. If his message was for the twelve only, then you and I who call ourselves preachers are out of the will of God. The twelve Apostles that Jesus chose were the first, not the last. The Bible calls Barnabas an apostle. Polycarp, who was taught in the gospel by the Apostle John, was an apostle. We are living in the age of the apostolic church. It can't be called apostolic if the apostles are dead. It would be "in memory to the Apostles". The title apostle means sent ones. Christ still sends us to the world. A disciple can be a woman, therefore a woman can preach.

(3)   Does God hear women disciples? If God hears preachers and a disciple is a preacher, then he hears women because a woman can be a disciple. St. John 17:20 "Neither pray I for these alone, but for them also which shall believe on me through their word:" A woman can be saved by believing on the name of the Lord. Jesus prayed that those who believed on him would be one with him. If they are one with him, then he hears them. God responds to faith as he did with Hannah in I Samuel 1:4-19. He will deliver his people when he sees faith. Here is the conclusion

of Hannah's faith. God heard her and sent Samuel as a deliver to His people. The people were saved from the enemy because God heard from a woman.

In these last days, the Disciples of Christ must proclaim the gospel to the world. God will hear and answer our prayers. He will work through us because we are his body. When a woman is saved and filled with the Spirit of God and then understands this in her heart, she will burn within. Oh how do we cry to the lukewarm church and the world from the spirit of John Bunyan, "Life, life, eternal life." (The Pilgrim's Progress, pg 19). We must put our finger in our ears to the world and declare, "I'm running for my life".

God and His Placement of Us in Authority

If we say that God does not place women in authority over men, then there should never be a time in history when a woman ruled over a man in the call of God. Whether it is a natural or a spiritual calling.

Romans 13:1-4 "Let every soul be subject unto the higher powers. For there is no power but of God: the powers that be are ordained of God. Whosoever therefore resisteth the power resisteth the ordinance of God: and they that resist shall receive to themselves damnation. For rulers are not terrors to good works, but to the evil. Wilt thou then not be afraid of the power? Do that which is good and thou shall have praise of the same: For he is the minister of God to thee for good. But if thou do that which is evil, be afraid: for he beareth not the sword in vain: for he is the minister of God, a revenger to execute wrath upon him that doeth evil.

Psalm 75:6-7 "For promotion cometh neither from the east, nor from the west, nor from the south. But God is the judge: he putteth down one, and setteth up another."

Daniel 2:21 "And he changed the times and the seasons: he removeth kings, and setteth up kings: he giveth wisdom unto the wise, and knowledge to them that know understanding."

Therefore, the queens of the Bible, and the queens that are listed in the history books (including all the modern day queens and leaders) were called of God. God placed them in authority over men. The Bible does not lie regarding the character of God. This means that the character of God is to place a woman in authority over a man:

The Queen of Sheba – I Kings 10th chapter.
Candice – Acts 8:26
Margaret Thatcher – Prime Minister of Great Britain
The Queens of England – The Queen Mother, Mary, Elizabeth and the others.
Lili'uokalani – Hawaii's Last Queen

They were and are called of God. These women were over the men of the world and men of God. There is no difference.

God is the author of all powers and dominions. The elevation to a place of authority comes from God. If a woman has been elevated to a place of God's authority then it has to be by the hand of God. Positions were made for humans. Humans were not made for positions. So then, it is up to us what we will do with them. They cannot do any thing for us. Jesus said, "The Sabbath was made for man, man was not made for the Sabbath."

What about the scripture in I Corinthians 14:34-40 "Let your women keep silence in the churches: for it is not permitted unto them to speak; but they are commanded to be under obedience, as also saith the law."

(1)   The subject of this context deals with speaking in tongues and prophesying. It deals with order in respect to speaking to the prophets while they address the church. The

custom of that day was for the Jewish women to keep silent in the synagogues, because they did not have an education. Their knowledge was limited as to how to ask questions. They could not read to recite the Holy Torah. – So the priests thought. Before renting any movie after you read this book, rent the movie Yentl. It is a wonderful true story about a young Jewish girl who dressed like a young boy to prove girls have brains and could read as well as men.

(2)   The church in Corinth had Corinthian women that were filled with the Holy Ghost. They were not of the Jewish culture where the women did not have an education. They had no training in the law of the elders. So when Paul stated they should be silent referring to the law, it was not the law of God. This practice was from man, not from God. There are no scriptures in the Bible that states women should keep silent in the church or in the synagogue. Jesus said man's traditions make the word of God of none effect. Mark 7th chapter. Whether it is Paul or Peter (including myself), we cannot make God's Church conform to the tradition of man and call it God.

(3)   There is no such law in the Old Testament commanding the women to keep silent in the local synagogue. However, there is a tradition

where the women sat silent on one side and the men sat on the other side of the synagogue. The synagogue is not the church because the church is not a building like the synagogue. All the laws and orders that pertained to the synagogue will be done away with as soon as there is an understanding of God's grace. The farther the apostles went from Judah, the more they saw changes in how people lived.

(4)   Paul was speaking to the wives. They should ask their husbands what the prophets said after the church service has dismissed. Quote mine "it is impossible to keep silent after God speaks to your spirit which has been renewed by the Holy Ghost." Paul is dealing with culture and order.

What about I Timothy 2:9-15? In the Hebrew Greek Key Study Bible, Spiros Zodhiates writes the following concerning Paul message to the women of the church. "To function properly, everything needs a person in the position of leadership, especially a family. The marriage unit consists of two people that have two distinct personalities. These two require a headship, and according to God's divine leadership ordinance, that would be the male. In I Timothy 2:11, there are several key words that show how a wife should convey a proper relationship to her husband. The first of these terms is *gune,* which depending on the context, may indicate a woman in general or a wife. The close relationship of this word with the word *andros,* meaning husband, not simply man requires that the word be translated <u>wife</u>. The subsequent term to consider is *hesuchia,* translated silence. In the New Testament it occurs numerous times referring to tranquility or the state of being undisturbed. This should be the understanding in this verse. One must bear in mind here that during the era of time when Paul was writing, it was usually men who were the ones to receive an education. If this word meant complete silence, women would never have the opportunity to ask questions or increase their knowledge of the Scriptures. Simply speaking, the wife ought to be displaying a tranquil spirit in her attempt to learn. The final word of key importance in understanding the silence mentioned in this verse is *hupotage,* meaning that to place in proper order, translated subjection. Paul wanted to express the ideal that in the wife's desire to learn; she should respect her husband's position over her in Christ (cf. Cor 11:3).

"The phrase in Timothy 2:12, But I suffer not a woman to teach…. should be understood as But I suffer not a wife to teach. The discussion continues drawing contrasts between the Greek words for wife and for husband. The usage of *gune* in this verse must be translated as a wife corresponding to the reference in verse eleven. However, *andros* is translated as man in verse twelve. However, it is better rendered husband when the usage of this Greek word occurs in relation to a discussion of wives. Furthermore, the word for teach in this verse is the Greek infinitive *didaskein*. In this instance, it means to teach continuously. The situation refers to the home, an assembly, or anywhere the husband and wife may be interacting together. If this were, the position of the husband as the head would be undermined, and would not be in accordance with God's ordained order in creation. A wife should place limitations on her speech. Paul does not want women to be lackluster or even mute, but to be careful lest they go beyond the bounds of accepted propriety."

Moreover, the word translated to <u>usurp authority over</u> is the Greek word **authentein.** Essentially, a wife's private or public life should be beyond reproach and never undermine the position that her husband has been given by God. Also, a wife should never encroach upon the role of her husband. In verse thirteen, Paul explains why this is so: "For Adam was first formed, then Eve." This is not because the husband is better, more worthy than she, but rather, it is the order originally ordained by God, for her to respect.

We can clearly see from this explanation that Paul is not saying a woman should not speak in the church. If this is the case then Paul clearly contradicted himself by telling the women to teach. Did he tell them to take the young women to their prospective homes to teach them, or teach them in a church setting? Titus 2:3-5 "The aged women likewise, that they be in behavior as becometh holiness, not false accusers, not given to much wine teachers of good things. That they may teach the young women to be sober to love their husbands, to love their children, to be discreet, chaste, keepers at home, good, obedient to their own husbands that the word of God be not blasphemed."

Most males do not understand what the church is. I will speak on this topic latter.

Who are the Sons of God? – Symbolic or Actual

God is a spirit and they that worship him much worship him in spirit and truth. John 4:24 "God is a Spirit: and they that worship him must worship in spirit and truth."

John 3:5 "Jesus answered, verily, verily, I say unto thee, except a man be born of water and of the Spirit, he cannot enter into the kingdom of God."

According to these scriptures it is the spirit of man that is born again. Jesus destroyed the nature of sin to give us the right to enter into a spiritual kingdom by being born again by his blood and of his spirit. We are his body. In Him there is neither male flesh nor female flesh. According to Romans 8th chapter we are in the Spirit.

Mark 12:25 "For when thy shall rise from the dead, they neither marry, nor are given in marriage; but are as the angels which are in heaven." What does the Bible say about angels? They are the sons of God. Angels are spirits. The church is a spiritual entity. We are in the church by the spirit; therefore, we are the sons of God. From a physical aspect, we are males and females, but by the spirit, we are sons.

God had only two sons that were of flesh; Adam and Jesus. Luke 1:35,38.

The unhappy thing about the information I am about to present is that man doesn't realize he isn't a child of God. We would like to act with sympathy to all human being and declare for conscience sake that all men are the children of God. That would make us all feel like we are one. Which in turn will remove any judgement of people's character, granting them the right to do as they will in the name of God. However, the truth of the matter is that the human race is the children of Adam. God gave Adam the procreative ability to replenish the earth. Inside of man (male and female) is an egg and a sperm, that creates protein and zygote, that creates a fetus (it has life, ears, eyes, limbs, a nose, a brain, and internal organs. However small they may be, they are there). The fetus cannot come into existence without the male and female getting together. God does not have to be in our lives for us to beget a child. You can be an atheist and children can be born unto you. That which is flesh is flesh. Every child that came into the world because of a miracle had a male sperm that penetrated a female egg. We are the children of men according to the flesh. However, if we have the spirit of God dwelling in us according to faith, we are the children of God. Romans 8th chapter and I John 3rd chapter.

So when women bashers say that God only uses sons – they don't have any knowledge about the church, and who are members of the church. Romans 8:14 "For as many as are led by the Spirit of God, they are the sons of God." They confuse the church with organizations. The church is about sonship. Sonship consist of sons; sons of God.

The Bride of Christ – Symbolic or Actual

The church is also considered brides/wives. If gender titles are used by God to indicate whom He will use in His Church, then He does not use men or the male genders. Brides/wives are women. No matter what era, or what country you study, a bride/wife is always a woman. In some countries, a man can be the husband of many wives at one time. The wives are females. So, is God saying only females are going to heaven, or is he conveying another message to us? God is conveying another message to us.

The church is the bride of Christ. Ephesians 5:32 "This is a great mystery: but I speak concerning Christ and the Church." The mystery is this, that the wife is symbolic to the church. She represents her husband like the church represents Christ. She has power in her husband's house, as the church has power over Christ house. The wife has her husband's name as the church has Christ's name. Here is a great mystery, the bride, being neither male nor female physically, is like the angels. They are spirits with power. Their desire is toward God. The wife's desire is toward her husband. Christ is coming to get his bride. The bride is neither male nor female. She is one spirit. The bride has been given power to rule the house with the spiritual gifts she has received from God; The bride – not man, not woman – but the bride.

God's bride is spiritual. She is neither male nor female. This is why the scripture declares in Galatians 3:23-29 that there is neither male nor female in Christ Jesus. In Matthew

59

25:1-12, Jesus is teaching the disciples about the coming kingdom and who will enter in. It is those who are pure and with wisdom watch for his coming.

In the physical part of the established church, we have many members and organizations. The physical church can establish any positions outside of the offices of apostles, prophets, evangelists, pastors, and teachers to ensure that the physical aspects of the church run efficiently. The physical church can include anyone or exclude anyone they wish from participating in the daily physical administration. They can tell a woman that she is excluded from preaching in the pulpits. They can stop her from working on the church grounds. They can stop her from participating in the government of the church, but they cannot stop her from preaching under the anointing of the Holy Ghost. The Bible tells us in I Thessalonians 5:19 not to quench the Holy Spirit of God.

What is the Bible saying to us regarding not quenching the Holy Spirit? The work of the Spirit is to be active in the children of God's lives. We are to spread the gospel of Jesus Christ through out the world. All of us are to be busy. If you notice after the Spirit of God fell in 30 AD, the disciples had more faith than they did before they came to Jerusalem. Therefore, we see by the changed life of the disciples that when a person has faith, they move by the power of the Holy Spirit. They are not to quench this Spirit. To whom is Paul writing? Is it the body of Christ, which includes women, or just the men? If he is talking to only men, then women do not even have the Holy Spirit. Paul is talking to the body of Christ; therefore, the women can be a part of that life-changing ministry.

The religious organizations that are owned by the religious heads can tell women that they are not permitted to do and be certain things in their churches. No one can demand the Papal Church to change its' stand on women in the priesthood. The church has the right to appoint who ever it will to certain positions. Now, if this were the Church of our Lord Jesus, then they would have to follow the guidelines of the Bible. No one can tell women in the Lord's church when they can or cannot preach.

The Lord's church is not about lifting weights, running miles, or ruling the world. It is not about being the head of the household. It is about preaching the gospel to the world. It is about perfecting the saints. "It is not by might nor by power, but my Spirit saith the Lord." Zechariah 4:6. We do not run this race by physical strength. It is by the help of God almighty. If this church was physical, like the nation of Israel, then women will not be appointed positions of strength. The male gender would be the heads. Nevertheless, the male gender is not the head of the church; Jesus Christ is the head of his church.

My question to the entire churches worldwide is, "who is your head?"

Franklin E. Rutledge

Are We One?

There are seven continents in the world: North America, South America, Africa, Asia, Australia, Europe, and Antarctica. Antarctica is the only uninhabited continent of the seven. The others have organized countries, states, cities, and towns, which is inhabited by people. These people have developed what we called cultures. The people in these cultures are linked to one race - the human race. Many good and bad practices have evolved over the years from these people. Each culture looks at the other's practices under a human judgmental microscope to determine if it can be of some assistance to bring the other up to *code*. Because of the Devil and human philosophy, people have divided themselves in different races of people. By war, each race has tried to conquer the other. This warring has created an attitude of separations, fears and prejudices. One race vaults itself over another then declares, "we are better than you, we are better than you." Jesus was born and died in this world to break down the walls that men have built to separate themselves.

The persecuted Church that is founded upon Jesus Christ has been given the task of marching behind these walls and declaring that God has made of one blood one people. Acts 17:26 "And hath made of one blood all nations of men for to dwell on all the face of the earth, and hath determined the times before appointed, and the bounds of their habitation;" All people will not believe this; therefore their hearts have to be changed. Acts 20:28 "Take heed therefore unto yourselves and to all the flock, over the which the Holy

62

Ghost hath made you overseers, to feed the church of God, which he hath purchased with his own blood." The Church is one. This emancipation proclamation must be given to everyone that accepts Jesus Christ as the sacrifice for his or her sins. Then and only then can we know that we are one. (1) One mind – Romans 12:1-4. (2) One body – Galatians 3:28, (3) and One hope –I Peter 3:7.

The old hymn goes, "We are one in the spirit, we are one in the Lord. We are one in the Spirit, we are one in the Lord…. And they will know we are Christians by our love, then they will know we are Christians by our love." Women that are saved are part of this. They are not a separate spiritual species that God will take with him after he comes and get these wonderful species called males.

To teach is to feed

(1)   To teach is to feed. The title of one who feeds God's people is a Pastor.

(2)   So, if a woman cannot pastor, she must not teach God's people in any capacity.

(3)   You do not have to be called a pastor to function in the office of a pastor. If women are allowed to teach, then they are being allowed to pastor.

(4)   If in time past God allowed a woman to hold an office that required her to be over men, whether it was his perfect or permissive will, she was in his will.

Isaiah 4:18 "The Spirit of the Lord is upon me, because he hath anointed me to preach the gospel to the poor; he hath sent me to heal the brokenhearted, to preach deliverance to the captives, and recovering of sight to the blind, to set at liberty them that are bruised."

Saints going to Hell because they listen to a woman

There are men preachers who believe that a child of God can be lost and go to hell because;

    (1)   they listen to a woman preacher

    (2)   they sit under a woman preacher or

    (3)   the woman herself is going to hell because she is the Pastor of a local assembly.

A saint of God cannot be condemned. How then can they go to hell for listening to a woman? (Romans 8:1). "There is therefore now no condemnation to them which are in Christ Jesus, who walk not after the flesh, but after the Spirit.... (9) But ye are not in the flesh, but in the Spirit, if so be that the Spirit of God dwell in you. Now if any man have not the Spirit of Christ, he is none of his.

Romans 8:31-39 – Nothing can separate us from the Love of God that is in Christ Jesus.

We are not saved by whom we listen to. We are saved by the sacrifice of God's Son. John 1:29 "Behold the Lamb of God that taketh away the sin of the world."

John 3:18 "He that believeth on him is not condemned: but he that believeth not is condemned already, because he hath not believed in the name of the only begotten Son of God."

Mark 16: "He that believeth and is baptized shall be saved"

The scriptures teach that we are saved by whom we believe in, not what we wear or who gives us the information. The scriptures do teach that we as saints should dress, act and speak as becoming people of the Most High God. It is our duty as people who have been saved from sin, not to be seen naked in public. For the saints, nakedness is a sin before God. Therefore, dressing is important but it is not what saves you.

Not listening to certain things is mentally and spiritually helpful, but it is not what saves you. The foundation of our salvation is the death, burial and resurrection of Jesus Christ. Everything else is material that is built on the foundation. It is not the foundation.

I John 3:9 "Whosoever is born of God doth not commit sin; for his seed remaineth in him; and he cannot sin, because he is born of God.

Mark 9:38-41 "And John answered him, saying Master, we saw one casting out devils in thy name, and he followeth not us: and we forbade him, because he followeth not us. But Jesus said, Forbid him not: for there is no man which shall do a miracle in my name, that can lightly speak evil of me. For he that is not against us is on our part. For whosoever shall give you a cup of water to drink in my name, because ye belong to Christ, verily I say unto you, he shall not lose his reward."

Philippians 1:15-18 "Some indeed preach Christ even of envy and strife: and some also of good will: The one preach Christ of contention, not sincerely, supposing to add affliction to my bonds: But the other of love, knowing that I am set for the defense of the gospel. What then? Notwithstanding, every way, whether in pretence, or in truth, Christ is preached: and I therein do rejoice, yea, and will rejoice."

I Corinthians 3:11-15 "For other foundation can no man lay than that is laid, which is Jesus Christ. Now if any man build upon this foundation gold, silver, precious stones, wood, hay, stubble; Every man's work shall be made manifest: for the day shall declare it, because it shall be revealed by fire; and the fire shall try every man's work of what sort it is. If any man's work abide which he hath built thereupon, he shall receive a reward. If any man's work shall be burned, he shall suffer loss: but he himself shall be saved: yet so as by fire.

This scripture clearly confirms that we will not be lost even if our works are burned. If a woman preaches in the name of Christ, but she is not supposed to, her works shall be lost, but she shall be saved. So, we better be careful how we testify that God said, but he did not say. We may be found false witness of God.

Preaching behind the podium on the pulpit issue

Many church organizations will not allow women preachers to stand on the pulpit. They will have them stand behind a podium on the lower lever of the church. This is how the churches in America during slavery treated the slaves. By putting them on the lower level, they hoped not to offend or disgrace God. What a bunch of garbage!

The church is not a brick and mortar building. It is not wood and metal. It does not have windows and pews with plush carpet or marble floors. Jesus said "upon this rock I will build my church, and the gates of hell shall not prevail against it." Matthew 16:18. The church is a spiritual kingdom. Ephesians 6:12 "For we wrestle not against flesh and blood, but against principalities, against powers, against the rulers of the darkness of this world, against spiritual wickedness in high places." John 18:36 "Jesus answered, My kingdom is not of this world: if my kingdom were of his world, then would my servants fight, that I should not be delivered to the Jews: but now is my kingdom not from hence."

The house of God is not what we call the house of God. Before Jesus was born, the house of God was made of wood and stones. It was very beautiful to look upon. People from all over the known world came to worship in it. From Moses to Solomon the temple of God was with men. Exodus 25:8 "And let them make me a sanctuary; that I may dwell among them. II Chronicles 7:12 "And the Lord appeared to Solomon by night, and said unto him, I have chosen this place to myself for an (a) house of sacrifice." Then after Solomon died, the temple was destroyed. God sent Ezra with the help of Zerubbabel and Nehemiah to rebuild the temple. The Romans came and with the help of the Pharisees made the house of God of no effect. Jesus ran them out of the temple and declared that it was the house of God. Luke 19:46 "…it is written, My house is the house of prayer: but ye have made it a den of thieves."

On the day that Jesus died, the veil in the temple was ripped from top to bottom. Matthew 27:51. This polluted the temple and the Spirit of the Lord left the building. In 70 A.D., the Roman army destroyed the beautiful Jewish temple. The Jews were dispersed over the known world. There were no more offering of lambs and the spreading of the ashes of the Red Heifer. God would completely abandon temples made with hands. Now he resides in those who have accepted His dear son Jesus Christ. I Corinthians 3:16-17 "Know ye not that you are the temple of God, and that the Spirit of God dwelleth in you? If any man defile the temple of God, him shall God destroy: for the temple of God is holy, which temple ye are." I Corinthians 6:19-20 What? Know ye not that your body is the temple of the Holy Ghost which is in you, which ye have of God, and ye are not your own? For ye are bought with a price: therefore glorify God in your body, and in your spirit, which are God's." II Corinthians 6:16 "And what agreement hath the temple of God with idols? For ye are the temple of the living God; as God hath said, I will dwell in them, and walk in them; and I will be their God, and they shall be my people." I Corinthians 3:9 "For we are labourers together with God: ye are God's husbandry, ye are God's building." Ephesians 2:20-21 "and are built upon the foundation of the apostles and prophets, Jesus Chris himself being the chief corner stone: In whom all the building fitly framed together groweth unto an holy temple in the Lord."

The spiritual church is now the building in which God dwells. No matter how small or large the building is where the church comes together, the Spirit of the Lord resides with the church. Jesus said "For where two or three are gathered together in my name, there I am in the midst" Matthew 18:20. Not where two or three men, or two or three women, or one man and two women, or one woman and two men, but human beings who believe in his name. This could be under a tree, inside a residential home, or Caesar's house, or in what we call a church building. By the way, do you know what the steeple on your church building (where women cannot pastor) represents? Read the book "The Two Babylon".

God is not interested in where a person stands when they deliver the word. His divine will is to deliver the word. It is so sad to see preachers fight about where a person will stand when they deliver the word of God to the people. I believe that what ever we dedicate to God it should be holy unto the Lord in our sight. We should not use those things without reverence; however, they should not be worshipped. All things in the house of prayer should be respected as unto the Lord. God is only in the place when the church is in the place.

I heard a story years ago about a man who went to visit a church that was <u>uptown</u>. The preacher always acknowledged the brother and thanked him for coming. One day the man wanted to join the church. The preacher said to him, brother I want you to pray and ask God if he wants you to join this church. This was done three times. So the man came back on a Sunday morning and the preacher asked the man, did God finally give you an answer? The man looked at the preacher and said, yes sir, the Lord told me not to join this church, because he cannot join this church. Therefore, pulpits are nothing but a place where you can be elevated above the people to whom you are speaking. Nehemiah 8:4 "And Ezra the scribe stood upon a pulpit of wood, which they had made for the purpose;.." It is just wood, or some other perishable material of which God is not concerned.

Maybe the women that God has given the gift of pastoring should leave some of the organizations that will not allow them to minister. I want to quote the apostles from Acts 4:18-19 "And they called them, and commanded them not to speak at all nor teach in the name of Jesus. But Peter and John answered and said unto them, whether it be right in the sight of God to hearken unto you more than unto God, judge ye." Acts 5:29, "Then Peter and other Apostles answered and said, we ought to obey God rather than men." Women, do not lose your rewards because of your surrounding male culture. Your head in the church is Jesus Christ. If you are a member in a local church, and you should be, you leader is the pastor of that church. Hebrews 13:17 "Obey them that have the rule over you, and submit yourselves: for they watch for your souls, they that must give account, that they may do it with joy, and not with grief: for that is unprofitable for you." The writer is speaking to every member in the local assembly. Within reason, we should obey man. This is only after we have come to know the voice of God.

Understand this – I Peter 5:2-4 "Feed the flock of God which is among you, taking the oversight thereof, not by constraint, but willingly; not for filthy lucre, but of a ready mind; Neither as being lords over God's heritage, but being ensamples to the flock. And when the chief Shepherd shall appear, ye shall receive a crown of glory that fadeth not away." Male leaders of the church are there to hear God, not to put in practice the action of their opinions. This is hard to do when you are insecure, and want to keep people under your rule. This is called bondage. In Luke 10:38-42 Jesus reminded Martha of what is most important to God. It was not cooking chicken dinners, or preparing a meal for the males of the house, it was worship. Martha was just obeying her culture. She was not allowed to participate in the things of God. Neither was Mary, but she obeyed her spirit and found the olive branch. Mary broke spiritual traditions, and was praise by God.

I was invited to speak at one of the local churches in Connecticut. The topic given to me was "a strong family makes a strong church." On the surface, it sounds correct and good. However, when I examined through prayer and meditated on the word of God what makes a strong family, I had to reverse this and say, "a strong church makes a strong family." St. John 15:1,4-5 "I AM the true vine, and my Father is the husbandman...Abide in me, and I in you. As the branch cannot bear fruit of itself, except it abide in the vine: no more can ye, except ye abide in me. I am the vine, ye are the branches: He that abideth in me, and I in him, the same bringth forth much fruit: for without me ye can do nothing." A family is only as strong as the substance pumped into it. The church is fed from God. You be the judge. Would you want the strength that comes from philosophy, or the strength that comes from God?

As I quoted from, Spiros Zodhiates earlier, Paul was speaking to husbands and wives regarding God's ordained order in the home. He is not speaking about headship in the spiritual church, because Christ, who is spirit, is the head of the church. The question from husbands is can the wife be a pastor in a church of which the husband is a member? Would not the wife be his head?

If God calls a woman into the pastoral ministry, she is not the head over her husband. The law of marriage never changes because of what a husband or wife does. If the husband cannot work because he is disable, and the wife is the sole financial provider in the home, that does not change the law of God. If he cannot give to her the financial stability that is required by culture, that should not lessen the wife's respect to her husband's God given authority. The wife cannot usurp authority over her husband, because of the order of God. "Wherefore they are no more twain, but one flesh. What therefore God hath joined together, let not man put asunder" (Matthew 19:6). The principle cannot be destroyed. The order cannot be destroyed. No one can destroy the institution of marriage. Divorce does not destroy the institution of marriage. It dissolves the marriage of the husband and wife that initiates the divorce.

73

If the wife is strong as Sarah or Jezebel, God's principle order cannot be broken. If the husband is as strong as Lamech or weak as Ahab, God's law of order remains the same. Therefore, the answer to the husbands' questions regarding God placing a wife as the pastor of a local church where her husband is a member is that God can, He has and He will. He is not violating His own order of husbands being the head of the wife. Marriage is marriage and the church is the church.

The most important thing men forget is the scripture in Colossians 1:18 "And he is the head of the body, the church: etc..." There is no head male or female over the body of Christ. We are all members, if we are in the body. I Corinthians 12:18,25 "But now hath God set the members every one of them in the body, as it hath pleased him...That there should be no schism in the body; but that the members should have the same care one for another."

The misconception about men being the heads of the church is that they completely ignore the scriptures, or think that their home is the church. This is far from the truth. The home is the husband's. The church is Christ's. The government states that if there is no husband in the house, then the woman is the head of the house. The government also declares that even if there is a man living with the woman, but not married to her, she is considered the head of the house. Headship has everything to do with marital status. This is in the natural, but not so with the church. Christ lives according to the Spirit. He is over his own house. Whether there are men present as members of the church or not, He is always the head. Hebrews 3:5-6, "And Moses verily was faithful in all his house, as a servant for a testimony of those things which are to be spoken after; But Christ as a son over his own house; whose house are we, if we hold fast the confidence and the rejoicing of the hope firm unto the end."

Therefore, the title of pastor may be given to a woman in the church. If she is married, she is still subject to her husband in his house. However, in the church, both of them are subject to Christ, and subject to the ministry under which they have been placed. He places in the body as it pleases him. If he wants to place a female as pastor, he does not have to get the husband's ok to do it.

Where did this doctrine come from?

Without condemning any, I hope to show how foolish this is.

Each one that names the name of Jesus Christ is to pray that the will of God be done in earth as it is in heaven (Matthew 6:10). The will of God has nothing to do with Christian organization's by-laws. God's ways are not our ways. He does as he pleases, when he pleases. He does not need the ok of <u>The Church That Has The Truth</u> to anoint a woman to preach. He is God. He has his own agenda. God's word is steadfast and sure. There are times when we read the word of God but don't know what it is saying. Then months or even years later, after reading it again, God reveals it unto us. No one church organization has the upper hand on understanding everything that is in the Bible (which is the word of God).

Here is a simple test of truth. Please read this scripture through before trying to understand it. Then quote it to the listening congregation at communion time.

I Corinthians 11:27 "Wherefore whosoever shall eat this bread, and drink this cup of the Lord unworthily, shall be guilty of the body and blood of the Lord." I have listen to sermon after sermon, from the least to the greatest of preachers, trying to explain how we had better not partake of the communion if there is unconfessed sin in our lives. Because, they say, sin will make us unworthy. This scripture is not dealing with the sin of the saints. It is dealing with proper attitude toward eating and drinking, while considering the body of Christ that is present to take thereof. Notice the adverb used to describe the verb eating. It is not an adjective that describes the noun, which would be the person that is eating. The Lord's Supper is about the person being remembered, not the person doing the remembering. Time prevents me from explaining what the Bible teaches about remembering His body.

Yes, as Christians we should not live with unconfessed sins in our lives. However, sins are dealt with in other places in the scriptures, not in the Lord's Supper. If you are a male pastor and has ever used the above, as a means of persuading people not to take communion because of the condition of their spiritual lives, then it is a possibility you might be wrong about women pastors as well. Study, meditation, prayer and an objective spiritual mind can help us conclude truth when we are dealing with the word of God. We cannot rip one page out of the Bible; waive it in the air and say, "here is the whole truth to the Word of God."

Christian Denominations that don't believe in Women Pastors

Do not be surprise at the number of Christian denominations that hold to a traditional non-biblical doctrine of not allowing a woman to pastor churches. Do not be surprise at the number of men pastors in Christian denominations that allow women to pastor, who do not believe in women pastors. Do not be surprise at the number of Christian women who do not believe in women pastors.

We really do have a right to our own opinion. We must be careful not to assume or presume when it relates to the oracles of God. Exodus 20:7 "Thou shall not take the name of the Lord in vain; for the Lord will not hold him guiltless that taketh his name in vain." Taken the Lord's name in vain means to bring God into agreement with us when we are wrong. For example, you are trying to persuade a person to believe you and you know that the word of God does not say what you are quoting, but you tell them God said it. This is taking the Lord's name in vain because you are bringing God in agreement with that which is not true. God cannot lie. God will not contract with a lie. Many times, we tell church members they should not do this or that because God said it, when God never said it. Pastor James Lee Beall writes in his study book, Laying The Foundation, "God warns us against presumption through the severe punishment He inflicted upon those who dare to presume upon Him. This word comes from the Latin *praesumere* which means "to anticipate, suppose, take in advance." The

English definition is much closer to the Bible usage; it means, "to dare, to take too much upon one's self."

"Presumption violates God's holiness and sovereign authority. Presumption openly defies God's right to choose people and places for His purposes. Those who presume take upon themselves authority that was not given to them. They overstep the limits of propriety and courtesy and intrude themselves into places where thy have no business."

And Nadab and Abihu, the sons of Aaron, took either of them his censer, and put fire therein, and put incense thereon, and offered strange fire before the Lord, which he commanded them not. And there went out fire from the LORD, and devoured them, and they died before the LORD (Leviticus 10:1,2)

We may assume something to be true when we don't have the facts. Assumption means the act of taking something for granted or supposing that a thing is true without basis in fact.

In 1997 I was sitting in one of our church council meetings, and I heard one of the women ministers shout out, "a woman should stay in a woman's place." My question to God was "what place is that." Soon after that, I was invited to do a seminar in a women's conference. My subject was "From Womanhood to Sainthood". It did not deliver married women from their marital responsibility. It fact it helped them to be better wives. The sainthood status elevated them to a greater place and responsibility than their counterparts that are in the world. There are saints, and there are women. Saints conform to the standards set by the word of God. Natural women conform to a philosophy that has no concrete standards in life. Today the standards are one thing, and then the next day they are another. The mentality of women is to do according to the philosophy of the world. The mentality of saints is to do according to the word of God.

Women in the church should be better wives, mothers and citizens because they live by a better standard. Even though non-church women can do virtuous things, women that fear the Lord shall excel above them all. Proverbs 31:29-31

Is God Male or Female?

God is neither male nor female. Male is a fleshly gender that has earthly limits and pleasures. Female is a fleshly gender that has earthly limits and pleasures. God is not fleshly and he has no limits. He is omnipresent, omnipotent and omnipotence. God is sovereign, and he is a spirit.

God is always referred to as He. The term he is a masculine pronoun that shows physical strength. The term she is a feminine pronoun that shows physical weakness. God is never weak, therefore is never referred to as she. God is referred to as a husband, and the church is referred to a wife. The husband is always a he, and the wife is always a she. God gives the seed (the word) to the church, and the husband gives the seed to the wife. God is He.

We are earthly. We must have earthly synonyms to compare with spiritual things, or the spiritual things will not make sense. St. John 3:12 "If I have told you earthly things, and ye believe not, how shall ye believe, if I tell you of heavenly things?" I Corinthians 15:46-47 "Howbeit that was not first which is spiritual, but that which is natural; and afterward that which is spiritual. The first man is of the earth, earthy: the second man is the Lord from heaven." I Corinthians 2:14 "But the natural man receiveth not the things of the Spirit of God: for they are foolishness unto him: neither can he know them, because they are spiritually discerned." God uses natural things to reveal himself to us. The human race that dwells in the carnal sense cannot understand the God of creation, but they can relate to carnality.

The attitude we have regarding the male and female place in the church is removed in this saying, there is neither male nor female in Christ Jesus. The church is to be run without gender or ethnicity. There are no Blacks, Whites, Reds, Americans, Indians, Russians, Chinese, Israelis, Arabs, and others in the church of the Lord Jesus Christ. Of course, the physical church has gender and ethnicity in it because the spirits that are saved dwell in these temples. We are many members but one body. Our attitude is one, not many. Any person that does not have this attitude needs to be born again by the word of God, or they are not in the church at all. We are one, or we are nothing at all. God has no stepchildren. Our understanding or lack of the word of God does not take away our oneness, if and only if Jesus Christ is the sacrifice for our sins.

God is a spirit. We are created physically in this aspect of the image of God. God is the head of the church – His wife. He is strong and powerful. Therefore, we must see him as "He". The only thing we have to symbolize him with in the natural is a male. He can never be referred to as she. She physically is the weaker vessel. God is not weak. Ah, the men will say. This is the answer. If the male represents the strength of God, this could resolve all the questions relating to who should be the leaders. Ah, I would reply. The church has a head. We quickly forget that there is neither male nor female in it. The male's physique is for the natural world. The physical bodies are for the pleasures of this world. Flesh and blood cannot inherit the kingdom of

Heaven, but "we", our spirits sit in heavenly places (Ephesians 1:3; 2:6; 3:7-10).

When speaking of the power of the Holy Spirit, we are speaking of the spiritual signs found in Mark 16. Katherine Kulhman was a woman in whom dwelled the Spirit of God. She was very powerful. Demons and diseases could not stand against her. Yet she had one of the smallest physical frames among the ministers that were used of God at that time. I am sure she could not participate in the heavy lifting that the men were involved in while putting up tents, but the real work was accomplished. That was casting out devils and healing the sick. The tent was an amenity. The church buildings were amenities. The power of the Holy Spirit worked in her not to put up tents, but to bring down the kingdom of the Devil. The same type of work Peter and John did in Acts 3:6-8, she did as well. We are fighting a spiritual battle with demons and devils (Ephesians 6:10-12).

If we were fighting a fleshly battle, we would be like the saints in the Old Testament. It would be one physical war after the other. Jesus said, my kingdom is not of this world: if my kingdom were of this world, then would my servants fight, that I should not be delivered to the Jews: but now is my kingdom not from hence" (John 18:36).

Franklin E. Rutledge

A Different Attitude

When man rule by a fleshly law, his laws changes based on his emotions. The Magna Carter changed by the will of the King. With each succeeding king, there came new laws and new ways of handling things. We do not know in what direction to go because the world keeps spinning and developing new ideals that are based on new discoveries. Aristotle did not believe that women, adults under 21 and slaves could understand philosophy. Hundreds of years later John Stuart Mill, a philosopher, brilliantly defended the capability of women to participate in government leadership.

It was believed that the African slaves could not read or write because they had no souls. However, in the 1800s we found out that they could read, even if they had to secretly obtain the education. George Washington Carver invented many things from the peanuts. The African American Slaves invented many of the medical operation procedures, automotive parts, the traffic light, the light bulb filament, and many other things. Some of this country's greatest statesmen are from that lineage. Now we have an African American Slave descendant as the Secretary of the United States. Boy what a contradiction! Just when you think you have things figured out in this life, new revelation comes along. The Professional Golf Association for many years did not allow descendant of American Slaves to play in their golf tournaments. Now you have Tiger Woods. I support Tiger in his description of his geno type, while understanding his pheno type with dark skin. However, the majority looks at him as a descendant of American slaves that came from Africa. Tiger is the greatest golfer today, and he has helped the PGA make millions in his short professional career. They said it couldn't be done. Well!!!!

Women of the European decent were not allowed to get a good education and participate in the high-level government. As John Stuart Mills augured, they are not only able to be highly educated but can run this country. Here are some excerpts from John Stuart Mill (1806-1873), The Subjection of Women.

Chapter III – Page 2, "And even if we could do without them, would it be consistent with justice to refuse to them their fair share of honour and distinction, or to deny to them the equal moral right of all human beings to choose their occupation (short of injury to others) according to their own preferences, at their own risk? Nor is the injustice confined to them: it is shared by those who are in a position to benefit by their services. To ordain that any kind of persons shall not be physicians, or shall not be advocates, or shall not be Members of Parliament, is to injure not them only, but all who employ physicians or advocates, or elect Members of Parliament, an who are deprived of the stimulating effect of greater competition on the exertions of the competitors, as well as restricted to a narrower range of individual choice."

Mill: Chapter III – Page 3, "Let us consider women only as they already are, or as they are known to have been: and the capacities which they have already practically shown, what they have done, that at least if nothing else it is proved that they can do. When we consider how sedulously they are all trained away from, instead of being trained towards, any of the occupations or objects reserved for men, it is evident that I am taking a very humble ground for them, when I rest their case on what they have actually achieved. For, in this case, negative evidence is worth little, while any positive evidence is conclusive. It cannot be inferred to be impossible that a woman should be a Homer, or an Aristotle, or a Michael Angelo, or a Beethoven, because no woman has yet actually produced works comparable to theirs in any of those lines of excellence. This negative fact at most leaves the question uncertain and open to psychological discussion. However, it is quite certain that a woman can be a Queen Elizabeth, or a Deborah, or a Joan of Arc, since this is not inference, but fact. Now it is curious consideration that the only things that the existing law excludes women from doing, are the things that they have proved that they are able to do. There is no law to prevent a woman from having written all the plays of Shakespeare, or composed all the operas of Mozart. But Queen Elizabeth or Queen Victoria, had they not inherited the throne, could not have been entrusted with the smallest of the political duties, of which the former showed herself equal to the greatest."

Mill: Chapter III – Page 5, "Let us consider the special nature of the mental capacities most characteristic of a woman of talent. They are all of a kind, which fits them for practice, and makes them tend towards it. What is meant by a woman's capacity of intuitive perception? It means a rapid and correct insight into present fact. It has nothing to do with general principles. Nobody ever perceived a scientific law of nature by intuition, nor arrived at a general rule of duty or prudence by it. These are results of slow and careful collection and comparison of experience; and neither the men nor the women of intuition usually shine in this department, unless, indeed, the experience necessary is such as they can acquire by themselves. For what is called their intuitive sagacity makes them peculiarly apt in gathering such general truths as can be collected from their individual means of observation."

Thank the Lord for America. In America, the slaves were taught how to pray to the Son of God, Jesus Christ. What the slave owners did not realized was that if you pray to the Lord Jesus Christ and believe in faith, He would answer. He did answer. The slaves were freed in 1863 under the Emancipation Proclamation Act. The European women prayed and God answered. The leaders of this country prayed before 1776 and God heard them. This country is free because someone prayed to the Lord.

The Bible states whom the Son make free they are free indeed. If Jesus Christ is the head of the church, then women will be free to do the will of God. Saved women should thank God that they live in America. You should thank God you do not live in a country where the religion is based on someone other than the Lord Jesus Christ.

The atheists thought they had the Christians between a rock and a hard place before the television and satellite were invented. They asked the question regarding Revelation 11:7-12, how can the whole world see two dead men come back alive? The answer to his question would come almost two thousand years later. God tricked them again.

Then make yourself the
object of every move without
an understanding

610-478-3455

ISA 57:13

Modern Day Women Pastors

There are women who live (d) in my time that have been very successful in the pastoral ministry. They have paved the way for other women that will come after them to be part of the ministry in general. These women have made many sacrifices to birth healthy ministries that are also the heart of the bloodline for some of our most *celebrated,* (no glory intended), ministers. Noel Jones started under Dr. Lulu Jackson. It would take volumes of books to tell of the many tangible spiritual accomplishments of women that have helped the physical church get to where it is today. I want to pay a small tribute to several women that have and/or are now pastoring local churches. These women had and do have a male-covering bishop over them.

Dr. Lulu Jackson: born October 17, 1907, in Cobbs, Georgia. At the age of 21, she was saved while attending a church service at the Emmanuel Church of Christ in Newark, New Jersey.

In 1937, the Lord sent her to Waterbury, Connecticut to establish a church in his name. She started the church in a rented storefront. Dr. Jackson with her husband and children by her side built the ministry under much sacrifice. The name of the church is Pentecostal Assembly Church. She had a church building constructed from the ground. She was later heard on W.A.T.R. radio station, and seen on Channel 13 in the greater Waterbury area, preaching and teaching the Word of God.

After a fire destroyed a previous building, the church purchased the building located at 39 Crown Street, where the church is presently located.

Dr. Lulu Jackson's ministry has taken her across the United States and into many foreign countries. A biographical sketch of her history has been published in the book entitle "Great Women of Pentecost". Under her leadership, many men and women were called to the pastoral ministry. One of the women called into the pastorate is currently the pastor of the church that was founded by Dr. Lulu Jackson.

Dr. Jackson never tried to act like a man or step in the place of a man. She soundly taught women preacher how to love their husband and take care of their children, while doing God's will. In the time and culture in which she lived, she would minister with all her might. But, she would respect the men that were over her.

Dr. Jackson served the Lord faithfully in words and deeds. She was well known throughout the world for her hard work and dedication to Lord. She was a member of the Pentecostal Assemblies of the World, Inc. In August of 1960, she was elected Vice President of the International Missionary and Women's Auxiliary. From 1964 to 1980, she served as President of the same auxiliary. She was the first woman to be elected to the Executive Bishop Board as Lay Director of the North East District. She served in the capacity for six (6) years over men who had the title of *bishop.*

At Dr. Jackson's funeral, a statement was made by First Lady Bowers (wife of former Presiding Bishop Paul A. Bowers) that summed up her leadership in the P.A. of W. *"If she was a man she would have been the Bishop."* I firmly agree. If she had been a man in her local council, she would have been the Council Chairman. She was a great vessel used of God.

Reverend Anne Gimenez: Co Pastor of Rock Church in Virginia Beach, Virginia. I do not know too much about this woman of God, but from what I know about the success of Rock Church in Virginia, she is called of God.

Joyce Meyer: The number one international Christian teacher. She is on more television stations, radio stations and church conferences than any other woman in the world. Her ministry has helped changed the lives of many people around the world. Her family, including her husband, has worked submissively and faithfully with her to bring the gospel of Jesus Christ to a world of hurting sick people. Joyce candidly talks about her character and attitude regarding her marriage and how she works on herself to please God and her husband. She teaches people to be real so they can repent and allow God to save them. She teaches Christians to be real so God can help them. I love listening to her because she speaks the language of real people. I think it would be advisable for all women to pay close attention to what she has to say. God bless you Joyce.

Pastor A. Ruth Williams: (11-29-?? to present). She is the current pastor of the Grace Apostolic Church of Jesus, Inc., Terryville, Connecticut. A member of the Pentecostal

Assembly of the World, Inc. Pastor Williams is from a family of 15 children. She is from the state of Tennessee. She is the daughter of the late Mr. and Mrs. Alexander Cross. She was saved while attending a church service at Bethesda Apostolic Church in New Britain, Connecticut; where the late Dr. John Shaw was the pastor. He also baptized her in the name of the Lord Jesus Christ.

Soon after her conversion, the Lord called her into the pastoral ministry. In the year 1952, she started her first work. The name of the church was Grace Apostle Church. Several families joined with her and the ministry began to grow. The Church worshipped in several locations before finally settling at 23 North Avenue in Terryville, Connecticut. The most talked about site was a building on Middle Street in Bristol, Connecticut. Many souls were saved at that location. Many ministries were birth out of that location. Across the New England region the saints are still sharing many, many wonderful memories of services that were held on Middle Street in Bristol, CT.

The church later moved to 23 North Avenue in Terryville, Connecticut. Years later the street was renamed Church Street. Pastor Williams and the Saints started worshipping in the basement of the house where she resided. Many souls were saved in that building, and the worshipers praised God to the point that the small room they occupied no longer seemed like it was small. Great testimonies of healing, deliverance, salvation and anointing to preach God's word have come out of this small church house. Pastor Williams married many couples in that small house church.

In 1975 Pastor Williams received a message from the Lord to build a larger church building next to the little house church. With only a small membership, and faith to trust God, she told the congregation and the District Council, that it was time to build and move out of this small worship place. Many of her fellow male ministers advised her not to do it because they could not see how God would allow her to do it. With the pressure from the male ministers and the fact that the congregation was small and poor, she heard from God again and sought to build. Ironically, the person that accepted the job was a male pastor that admittedly opposed women pastors; to the point that he believed that a person would go to hell if they helped or listen to a woman preacher. With little money, a faithful congregation, a secret friend that donated and many sacrifices from the members of the church, the building went up.

On October 30, 1982, the Grace Apostolic Church of Jesus, Inc. dedicated the building unto the Lord. The corner stone was set and dedicated on October 27, 1984.

Today, at the end of Church Street in Terryville, there is a beautiful church building erected because (I believe) God was leading this woman. The church's motto is "this is the church that faith built."

Pastor Williams is a hard working saint of God who has dedicated her life to the ministry in which God has given to her. She had to face many obstacles from men and her health. But as the Apostle Paul testified to the King, "having obtained help from God I continued unto this day." There were many men pastors that wanted to preach to her congregation, but did not want her to preach to their congregations. She prevailed by the power of the Holy Spirit and many people were saved and blessed by the messages that God had given her. She never tried to prove that God called her into the ministry; she just worked while being lead by God.

She had many physical problems and illnesses, but she never allowed these to hinder her from doing the will of God. She has had pneumonia at least seven times, and at least three strokes. But, through prayer she prevailed to do the work of God. Many leaders would have given up this burdensome work, but she stayed on course.

Pastor Williams is a praying woman, and she believes that prayer works above everything that we can do in the Lord. The motto that others have labeled her with is "Pray darling". Many people seek her for wise counsel. She is a blessing to all of God's people.

Many preachers in the Connecticut District Council and other organizations preached their first message/sermon, and their first revival in the church where she pastors. Everyone that has preached in her assembly can testify that preaching is made easy when you are preaching in Terryville. Many pastors received their calling because of being in and under her ministry.

Even though the congregation where she pastor is small, it is one of the most stable churches in the Connecticut

District Council, P.A. of W., Inc. Pastor Williams is a person who shows love and concern for all people. The members of the congregation portray this same spirit. The worship service is long remembered by most saints that enter into the sanctuary. Because of the spirit filled attitude of worship, most preachers that have ever preached at Grace Apostolic Church testifies that this is the easiest church to preach in. This statement is a testimony to the freedom of the Holy Spirit.

Pastor Williams is a faithful servant of God. She is a testimony to the scripture in Hebrews 10:25 "Not forsaking the assembling of ourselves together, as the manner of some is; but much the more, as ye see the day approaching." She currently has to be pushed in a wheelchair from the parsonage to the church. Her health is failing, but she never misses a church service. She cannot physically preach any more, but she continues to teach bible class. Her very presence encourages the saints to attend services regularly. Even though her body is failing her, her mind is as strong as ever. This woman is the epitome of faithfulness.

When we have our District Council meetings, she attends faithfully while being pushed in her wheelchair. One of the preachers who do not believe in women pastors said, "if God called any woman to pastor, he called Pastor Williams." As I indicated in one of my earlier chapters, no circumstance can establish the truth of God. It has to be God and God alone that determines whether He calls a woman to pastor. I believe, based on my understanding of the scriptures, that A. Ruth Williams is called and anointed of God to pastor His flock in the city of Terryville, Connecticut.

From September 1,2002 through September 8,2002, the Church celebrated Pastor Williams' 50th Pastoral Anniversary. May God continue to bless you Pastor Williams!

Geography doesn't change God's law of Holiness

Monotheism speaks of the oneness of God. God is one. Deuteronomy 6:1-4 "Now these are the commandments, the statutes, and the judgments, which the Lord your God commanded to teach you, that ye might do them in the land whither ye go to possess it:…. Hear, O Israel: The Lord our God is one Lord." Throughout Israel's history God kept reminding the children of Israel that there was no other God beside him, and that He is one. He changes not. We do not always understand his ways. If we think we do we are only fooling ourselves. He is the same yesterday, today, and forever more. For us to say these words and then change our dress style, our organization's by-laws based on the changing times, is to say that we do not believe that God cannot change. On the other hand, the things we changed from are not things God is concerned with in the first place. As the miter and the lava changed with events and times during Israel's history, so sanctification codes changed with the event and time of the church. But, the one thing that can never change is "Holiness unto the Lord."

In each continent, country and state, we have a different culture: the food we eat, the color clothing that we wear, the type of clothing we wear, the dialect we speak, the places we go, the access to higher education, and for some the mode of transportation that is used. If a nation of people wear hats, will that change or violate the will of God for another nation? If a people wear dark color clothing, does that mean that all have to wear dark color clothing? It is essential for us to understand that God does not judge or reward us for the necessary practices of our cultures. However, God's law is the same for all nations and people (Acts 2:37-39). God changes not.

God does not allow or disallow women to minister because of our established cultures. If he called Priscilla of Italy, very well learned in the scriptures, he can also call a woman in America. If he does not call women to the ministry, all the women missionaries are out of the will of God and cannot prosper. He changes not. We have to separate our church culture from the commands and will of God. Many of the things we hold as "God's law", are no more than our personal conviction and subjective practices. Many times leaders hold the people captive because they are afraid of their own weaknesses. Do not wear this. Do not wear that. Do not wear gold, or silver, or red or blue. Some men pastors go as far to say do not drive certain cars. If a person works hard and earns enough money to buy a luxurious car, they should not be told not to buy the thing because the pastor of the congregation came from a humble *abode.* If the pastor of that assembly states God is against having luxurious things, he or she is taking the Lord's name in vain.

Church culture is a very touchy issue. One of my favorite preachers in the late 1970's was Dr. John R Rich. In his monthly magazine, he would talk about standards for holy people. He spoke to the conscience of the people of God to build their confidence, to be the people of God, to bring people to Christ (not just him, but his writers as well).

His message to the saints was this, you are, and therefore you should dress. He addressed the issue of wearing jewelry, neckties, women pants and dresses, cutting of hair and polishing the fingernails. But I do not remember him saying it was God's law. If it is God's law then time must never change how we dress. We must all do the same things, regardless of the country and times in which we live. If we don't all dress and wear our hair the same way, we are still in our sins. Thank God, for the Blood of Jesus that washed away our sin.

Can you imaging the poor black women in the remote places of Africa who have short hair. What if God judged those women by their short hair? None could be saved. Just imagine if God judged car-drivers based on the people who believe that horses and buggies are the way to go. Some church leaders do not believe in computers. Some do not believe in airplanes. They say, "If God wanted us to fly he would have given us wings." Listen dear souls, we are not flying, the airplane is flying. We are riding inside of the flying airplane. God never intended for us to fly. He has not changed. The law of gravity demands that we never fly. Our personal belief not mixed with wisdom can destroy the spirit of a person who is seeking the delivering power of the Holy Ghost.

The Church is like no other body of people. Her head is the Lord Jesus Christ. He can not be seen with the nature eye. He works through the spirits of those that are members of his body. He feeds only the spirit of those who trust him for salvation. No one should lord over his body, because his body has a Lord. That lord is the Lord. Therefore, the blood of Jesus is not demographic-related to areas. It is universal. That law and that law only is what the people with their worldwide cultures must obey. If and only if a habit is spelled out in the Bible as sinful, must the people reject that habit and conform to the law of grace.

We cannot do away with church standards and the things that pertain to holiness. We just put them in their rightful place; after salvation.

The Church of the Lord Jesus Christ does not have a Pope. It does not have Prelate. It does not have a Watch Tower. It does not have a statue of a fat man. It does not have a General Superintendent. It does not have a conceived spiritual being by the name of Moroni. It has the Lord for its' head. No one can set laws for the Church. I do not wish to insult any religion or religious organization, because I am part of a church organization, but we should all understand that the Bible is the Christian Church's guideline. The religious organizations can do as they wish with their members. They can allow a woman to participate or not. If the Catholic Church wishes to bar women from their priesthood, they have that right because the laws of that church come from the Pope. He is the head of that church. Muslims can refuse women from taking part in their ministry, because they created it. The Jehovah's Witness can exclude women from the administration of elders, because Charles Russell and Joseph Rutherford started that religion. All the religions of the world can do as they please with women, because of their foundation.

All of the Christian denominations, including non-denominations, which accept Jesus Christ as its head, only have one law. That law is the Holy Bible. That law is the law of grace. It tells children to obey their parents in the Lord. It tells wives to obey your husbands in the Lord. It tells men to love your wives as Christ loved the Church. The Apostles made a foundational statement for all the members of the Church, "we will obey God over man."

If any Christian denomination will not allow a member of Christ's body to work according to the election of his grace, then that member should resign from that organization. No Christian women should be held hostage where Jesus Christ has set them free. Christian women, the Bible tells us to obey them that have the rule over us, for they watch for our soul. However, this obedience is in the Lord. Your job is to proclaim the message of Jesus Christ. Do not be fooled. God is not mocked. Whatsoever a man sows that shall he also reap.

If any Christian will conclude that God did not call a Christian woman to pastor His church, they must disprove the following:

A. Jesus Christ is the head of Church.
B. The Church is spiritual.
C. That we join the Church by a spiritual transformation.
D. That the spiritual gifts given to the Church are for all in the Church.
E. That we are one in Christ Jesus.
F. That it is our spirits that are anointed.

Conclusion: The members of the body of Christ must preach Christ in the entire world. The head of the body is Christ; he places in his body as it pleases him. He is not concerned with whether it pleases the male. Moreover, if a woman is in error because she pastors a local church assembly, God is still glorified.

The women in God's Church cannot be subjected to the qualification that secular organizations are. They are under the grace of God, as are men, to perform the will of God. Time does not permit me to write in this book, how Christian women should treat their husbands and children, if they have any. However, every Christian woman should consider a relationship with God first before she considers one with a man. God is the only one that knows how to bind you, but give you freedom at the same time.

Even in the natural world, women must declare that they have a brain, and that their God given ability can be exercised through the writing of books, heading of nations, leading television talk show hosts, and deans of colleges. Especially in America where we believe in the truth of our motto, "one nation under God." We also believe that this God is none other than the Lord Jesus Christ, who has stated that, "If the Son sets you free you shall be free indeed." Therefore, by this testimony the women in this country are free. I encourage every Christian woman that have been saved from sin and planted in the kingdom of His dear Son, to hear from God before entering into the gospel ministry. This is not like managing a great corporation, this is fighting unseen spirits. Moreover, I encourage every woman in this great land of the free and home of the brave, to continuing seeking to be President of this United States of America. God may select Mrs. Hillary Rodham Clinton or Mrs. Elizabeth Dole to be the next president after President Bush. God does not need my permission to set kings in office. He selected William Jefferson Clinton. How many of us believe that the Florida miscount was a fluke. It was the plan of God. The American people said we want Al Gore. I have nothing bad to say about the man. However, God said I want George W. Bush. The grace of God passes all understanding. If you want to challenge me on this, you can, but as a Bible believing person you must believe God sets kings in office. If you are not a Bible believing person, you have no voice. God knows exactly whom he wants in that position, we just have to vote to perform our civil duty. St. John 11:49-51, "And one of them, named Caiaphas, being the high priest that same year, said unto them, Ye know nothing at all. Nor consider that it is expedient for us, that one man should die for the people, and that the whole nation perish not. *And this spake he not of himself: but being high priest that year, he prophesied that Jesus should die for the nation;"* Caiaphas was against Jesus, but God used him as he pleased. He is the potter, and we are the clay.

As the gospel song goes, "What God has for you it is for you." No one can stop God from doing what he wants to in your life, no not even you. (St. Luke 1:5-25).

Franklin E. Rutledge

About the Author

Franklin Edward Rutledge. Born in the town of Wilton, Alabama. The sixth of twelve children from the deceased parents Forrest Freeman Rutledge and Ola Mae Fitts Rutledge. He is an ordained elder of the Pentecostal Assemblies of the World, Inc. He is an elder at the Grace Apostolic Church of Jesus in Terryville, Connecticut. He served 4 years in the United States Military. He's currently studying psychology at Central Connecticut State University as a part time student. He is dedicated to the true interpretation of God's word.